THE REVIEW *of* CONTEMPORARY FICTION

THE EDITIONS P.O.L NUMBER

FALL 2010 | VOL. XXX, NO. 3

EDITOR

JOHN O'BRIEN

ASSOCIATE EDITORS

MARTIN RIKER

IRVING MALIN

GUEST EDITOR

WARREN MOTTE

MANAGING EDITOR

JEREMY M. DAVIES

BOOK REVIEW EDITORS

LINDSEY DRAGER

JEFFREY ZUCKERMAN

PRODUCTION

JESSICA HENRICHS

PROOFREADER

ELLEN HORNOR

REVIEW OF CONTEMPORARY FICTION
Fall 2010
Vol. XXX, No. 3

The *Review of Contemporary Fiction* is published three times each year
(March, August, November). Subscription prices are as follows:

Single volume (three issues):
Individuals: $17.00 U.S.; $22.60 Canada; $32.60 all other countries
Institutions: $26.00 U.S.; $31.60 Canada; $41.60 all other countries

ISSN: 0276-0045
ISBN: 978-1-56478-615-9

Partially funded by the University of Illinois at Urbana-Champaign and by a grant from the
Illinois Arts Council, a state agency.

Indexed in *Humanities International Complete, International Bibliography of Periodical Literature, International Bibliography of Book Reviews, MLA Bibliography,* and *Book Review Index.*
Abstracted in *Abstracts of English Studies.*

The *Review of Contemporary Fiction* is also available on 16mm microfilm, 35mm microfilm, and
105mm microfiche from University Microfilms International, 300 North Zeeb Road, Ann Arbor,
MI 48106-1346.

Address all correspondence to:
Review of Contemporary Fiction
University of Illinois
1805 S. Wright Street, MC-011
Champaign, IL 61820

www.dalkeyarchive.com

THE REVIEW OF CONTEMPORARY FICTION

BACK ISSUES AVAILABLE

Back issues are still available for the following numbers of the
Review of Contemporary Fiction ($8 each unless otherwise noted):

William Eastlake / Aidan Higgins
William S. Burroughs ($15)
Camilo José Cela
Chandler Brossard
Samuel Beckett
Claude Ollier / Carlos Fuentes
Joseph McElroy
John Barth / David Markson
Donald Barthelme / Toby Olson
William H. Gass / Manuel Puig
José Donoso / Jerome Charyn
William T. Vollmann / Susan Daitch /
    David Foster Wallace ($15)
Angela Carter / Tadeusz Konwicki
Stanley Elkin / Alasdair Gray
Brigid Brophy / Robert Creeley /
    Osman Lins
Edmund White / Samuel R. Delany
Mario Vargas Llosa / Josef Škvorecký
Wilson Harris / Alan Burns
Raymond Queneau / Carole Maso
Curtis White / Milorad Pavić
Edward Sanders
Writers on Writing: The Best of The *Review of
    Contemporary Fiction*
Bradford Morrow
Henry Green / James Kelman / Ariel Dorfman
David Antin
Janice Galloway / Thomas Bernhard / Robert
    Steiner / Elizabeth Bowen

Gilbert Sorrentino / William Gaddis /
    Mary Caponegro / Margery Latimer
Italo Calvino / Ursule Molinaro /
    B. S. Johnson
Louis Zukofsky / Nicholas Mosley /
    Coleman Dowell
Casebook Study of Gilbert
    Sorrentino's *Imaginative Qualities of
    Actual Things*
Rick Moody / Ann Quin /
    Silas Flannery
Diane Williams / Aidan Higgins /
    Patricia Eakins
Douglas Glover / Blaise Cendrars /
    Severo Sarduy
Robert Creeley / Louis-Ferdinand Céline /
    Janet Frame
William H. Gass
Gert Jonke / Kazuo Ishiguro /
    Emily Holmes Coleman
William H. Gass / Robert Lowry /
    Ross Feld
Flann O'Brien / Guy Davenport /
    Aldous Huxley
Steven Millhauser
William Eastlake / Julieta Campos /
    Jane Bowles

NOVELIST AS CRITIC: Essays by Garrett, Barth, Sorrentino, Wallace, Ollier, Brooke-Rose, Creeley, Mathews, Kelly, Abbott, West, McCourt, McGonigle, and McCarthy
NEW FINNISH FICTION: Fiction by Eskelinen, Jäntti, Kontio, Krohn, Paltto, Sairanen, Selo, Siekkinen, Sund, and Valkeapää
NEW ITALIAN FICTION: Interviews and fiction by Malerba, Tabucchi, Zanotto, Ferrucci, Busi, Corti, Rasy, Cherchi, Balduino, Ceresa, Capriolo, Carrera, Valesio, and Gramigna
NEW DANISH FICTION: Fiction by Brøgger, Høeg, Andersen, Grøndahl, Holst, Jensen, Thorup, Michael, Sibast, Ryum, Lynggaard, Grønfeldt, Willumsen, and Holm
NEW LATVIAN FICTION: Fiction by Ikstena, Bankovskis, Berelis, Kolmanis, Ziedonis, and others
THE FUTURE OF FICTION: Essays by Birkerts, Caponegro, Franzen, Galloway, Maso, Morrow, Vollmann, White, and others ($15)
NEW JAPANESE FICTION: Interviews and fiction by Ohara, Shimada, Shono, Takahashi, Tsutsui, McCaffery, Gregory, Kotani, Tatsumi, Koshikawa, and others
NEW CUBAN FICTION: Fiction by Ponte, Mejides, Aguilar, Bahr, Curbelo, Plasencia, Serova, and others
SPECIAL FICTION ISSUE: JUAN EMAR: Fiction and illustrations by Juan Emar, translated by Daniel Borzutzky
NEW AUSTRALIAN FICTION: Fiction by Murnane, Tsiolkas, Falconer, Wilding, Bird, Yu, and others
NEW CATALAN FICTION: Fiction by Rodoreda, Espriu, Ibarz, Monsó, Serra, Moliner, Serés, and others
NEW WRITING ON WRITING: Essays by Gail Scott, William H. Gass, Gert Jonke, Nicholas Delbanco, and others
GEORGES PEREC ISSUE: Essays by Perec, Harry Mathews, David Bellos, Marcel Bénabou, and others
SPECIAL FICTION ISSUE: *; OR THE WHALE*: Radically abridged *Moby-Dick*, edited by Damion Searls
WRITING FROM POSTCOMMUNIST ROMANIA: Fiction and essays by Andrei Codrescu, Dumitru Tsepeneag, Mircea Cartarescu, and others
SLOVAK FICTION: Fiction by Johanides, Juráňová, Kapitáňová, Karvaš, Kompaníková, and others

Individuals receive a 10% discount on orders of one issue and a
20% discount on orders of two or more issues. To place an order,
use the form on the last page of this issue.

CONTENTS

THE REVIEW *of* CONTEMPORARY FICTION

INTRODUCTION: WHY P.O.L MATTERS

The first premise of this volume is that the Parisian publishing house known as the Editions P.O.L deserves the attention of *The Review of Contemporary Fiction*'s readers. It is prudent, I think, to articulate that premise, tempted though one might be to leave it as a tacit given. When it is a question of literature, of its uses and its fate, very little can be taken for granted these days—and surely not an American reader's interest in a French publisher. That being said, it seems to me that the people who turn to the *Review* are not garden-variety readers. Granted the territory that the *Review* has staked out over the years, it is legitimate to suppose that those people are inquisitive folk, people who are willing to try new flavors of fiction, and eager to learn what might be going on outside of their own neighborhood. More particularly still, I imagine them to be champions of what John O'Brien has called "subversive literature," or books that take a critical stance with regard to the canon and its conventions.

Readers of that sort, gazing across the Atlantic, will easily recognize that many of the experiments which shaped progressive literature and led it forward in the West during the last century and a half or so (from, say, Baudelaire and Mallarmé through the Theater of the Absurd and the New Novel) were conducted in France. Although the notion of the avant-garde is now largely exhausted, during the many years of its currency one of the avant-garde's epicenters was most certainly Paris. It was a place where art was taken seriously. Literature most especially put itself to the question there, again and again, in a continual effort to make something new. That impulse, which is at present largely moribund in the literary mainstream, is to the contrary very much alive at the Editions P.O.L—and that is chiefly why P.O.L matters.

P.O.L is spelled with two periods and no hyphen. Let me be clear about that, if about nothing else. I confess that I have difficulty remembering to spell it that way, and I'll wager that I'm not alone. One might expect it to be spelled differently, granted the name of its founder, from whom the publishing house is practically inseparable. Paul Otchakovsky-Laurens came up through the ranks of French publishing. Born in 1944, he studied law at the university, and then apprenticed at the Éditions Christian Bourgois before moving to Flammarion in 1970 as a series editor, and later to Hachette (in 1977), where he created a series under his own imprint. In 1983, he set up shop on his own, establishing the Editions P.O.L, and enlisting therein some of the most innovative young writers he had worked with at Flammarion and Hachette, figures such as Georges Perec, René Belletto, Renaud Camus, Leslie Kaplan, and Marc Cholodenko. In the years since then, he has built a catalogue known for its boldness and its originality. Along the way, Otchakovsky-Laurens himself has acquired a reputation as a singularly open and inquiring reader, one who is willing to promote intriguing writerly work wherever he may find it. Though not himself a writer, it can be argued that his initiatives have helped to set the terms for contemporary French literature in significant ways. He can thus already take his place in the pantheon of modern French publishing, alongside figures like Gaston Gallimard, Jean Paulhan, and Jérôme Lindon, people who had the good fortune to work in periods more heroic than his, and ours.

The Editions P.O.L cannot be said to have a "signature style," unlike what has on occasion been claimed about other French publishing houses (and notably the Editions de Minuit under the direction of Lindon). Quite to the contrary, its catalogue is impressively diverse and nonsectarian. It has been that way from the outset, moreover. The director has made it clear that decisions to publish are his alone—there is no editorial committee at P.O.L—and that they are largely based on personal taste. "I don't look for books that sell," Otchakovsky-Laurens says, "rather, I try to sell books that appeal to me." Certain of those books have sold very well indeed, enough in any case to keep the house a viable one in an increasingly difficult marketplace. Marguerite Duras's *La Douleur* (*The War*, 1985), a pungent text delicately mixing memoir and autofiction, was an early success, selling one hundred thousand copies, a more than respectable figure for a newly founded venture. Marie Darrieussecq's *Truismes* (*Pig Tales*), a story that takes its place in metamorphosis narratives from Ovid to Kafka, followed in 1996. It sold 240,000 copies in the original edition; 160,000 more in paperback; and elicited translations in thirty-five different countries. Martin Winckler's novel *La Maladie de Sachs* (*The Case of Doctor Sachs*), which appeared just two years later, sold a quarter of a million copies. The prestigious Prix Goncourt was finally awarded to a P.O.L book in 2008 for Atiq Rahimi's *Syngué sabour: Pierre de patience* (*The Patience Stone*), a novel focusing on violence and suffering, and narrated by a Muslim woman. Like the National Book Award or the Booker Prize (but still more so, as it were), the Goncourt guarantees immediate notoriety, exceptionally broad sales, and international interest.

Among all of those success stories, the real success of the Editions P.O.L is undoubtedly elsewhere. It may become apparent when one casts a sustained, critical glance on P.O.L's catalogue; or one may appreciate it in a more local reflection, one focused on individual writers. What I am trying to get at here is, on the one hand, the way P.O.L has welcomed richly challenging literature into its fold and, on the other, the manner in which it has provided a home for serious, deeply committed writers who might otherwise have been left to wander. It is difficult to imagine a catalogue as richly varied as theirs, one that puts on offer challenging, innovative poets like Pierre Alferi, Olivier Cadiot, Emmanuel Hocquard, and Dominique Fourcade, right alongside trenchant participatory journalists and polemicists such as Jean Rolin and Mathieu Lindon. Or where the pleasingly disengaged, lapidary essays of Marc Le Bot rub elbows with carefully crafted explorations of the material world, like the texts of Leslie Kaplan. Where a riotously comic novel such as Iegor Gran's *Acné festival* (1999) takes its place beside a more sober meditation on loss and loneliness like Patrick Lapeyre's *L'Homme-sœur* (Sister-Man, 2004). Where François Matton's delicate graphic images in books like *Sous tes yeux* (Right in Front of You, 2008), accessible to anyone willing to contemplate them, sit next to Katalin Molnár's *quant à je (kantaje)* [as to I (astooeye)] (1996), an arduous, hermetic text entailing responsibilities that many readers will find too onerous.

The very heterogeneity of P.O.L's catalogue can be taken, I think, as one of the publisher's defining characteristics. In a lengthy interview devoted to the Editions P.O.L, Marie Darrieussecq locates the exceptionalism of the house squarely in the personality of its director: "That may explain why such radical choices are made at the Editions P.O.L, choices that can provoke radical reactions. It's one man alone who makes decisions, with his subjectivity. There is no flaccid and deplorable system like that of certain other publishers, where everything new resembles everything else." Over the years, Otchakovsky-Laurens has acquired the reputation of someone quick to recognize literary merit, and that of an advocate willing to let writers follow their muse. His greatest early coup in that sense was surely his promotion of Georges Perec, a figure whom many critics now feel to be the most intriguing French writer of his generation. Otchakovsky-Laurens recruited Perec to his series at Hachette in the late 1970s, publishing four of his books there. *La Vie mode d'emploi* (*Life A User's Manual*) won the Prix Médicis in 1978, and helped to secure a far broader audience than Perec had enjoyed up until that point. Without a doubt, Georges Perec would have been one of the pillars of the Editions P.O.L, had he not died shortly before the house was founded. (Indeed, the logo that Otchakovsky-Laurens chose for his new enterprise, four black stones and three white, representing the "eternity" position from the Japanese game of *go*, was an image dear to Perec, and one that he used in his novel.) Such a reputation for intrepidity and discernment has clearly served Otchakovsky-Laurens well. Darrieussecq herself mentions that when she went looking for a publisher some twenty years later, she chose him because, "He published *Life A User's Manual*. The Vasco da Gama of literature." That advocacy of innovative writing has continued unabated over the years. And it is abundantly apparent right now, granted P.O.L's energetic promotion of gifted and original writers such as Christine Montalbetti, whose astonishing novels confirm the vigor of a genre many thought to be staggering toward its dotage.

Among all of the many editorial gestures one might point toward in an effort to describe the particularity of the Editions P.O.L, three seem to me particularly exemplary, and I would like briefly to underscore them here. The first one involves the writer Jacques Jouet. One of the most consistently original and refreshing figures in contemporary French literature, Jouet is someone who resists easy classification. He has worked in a broad variety of literary genres—verse, theater, novel, short story, essay, and so forth, even upon occasion trying his hand at lexicography—as if in an effort to traverse the spectrum of literary possibility. Having inaugurated his career in 1978 with a book entitled *Guerre froide, mère froide* (Cold War, Cold Mother), Jouet's work appeared at almost twenty different publishing houses before he finally came to roost at P.O.L in 1998. He was welcomed there with an extraordinary token of editorial confidence: the publication of a three-volume collection of poetry entitled *Navet, linge, oeil-de-vieux* (Turnip, Cloth, Old-man's-eye). That text, all 938 pages of it, can be read in many ways. First and foremost however, one must see in it an unconditional affirmation of the vitality of poetry as a cultural practice deeply embedded in the fabric of everyday life. Beginning in April of 1992, Jouet had decided to write a poem a day, whatever other writing tasks he might be engaged in; *Navet* records the first four years of that experiment. There are lots of different kinds of poems. Some are short, a few comprising only one word. Some are long, including a poem Jouet returns to periodically over the four-year period, written in alexandrines and terza rima, with an internal rhyme scheme he calls "rime berrychonne" (after the American poet John Berryman), which includes 4002 lines. There are poems on the still-life that lends its title to the collection, and which Jouet kept on his desk during those years, composed of a turnip, a linen napkin, and an "old man's eye" (a clear, square, biconcave lens used by landscape painters). There are occasional poems, free-verse poems, and fixed-form poems (such as the "morale élémentaire," a form elaborated by Raymond Queneau). There are "metro poems," composed according to a constraint which dictates that each verse must be composed between the various stations of a trip on the Parisian subway. There are examples of a form Jouet calls the "addressed poem," that is, a poem written with a certain person in mind, playing in some manner upon that person's name, and intended—initially at least—for that person alone. There are, finally, many poems on painting here, and indeed the collection is dedicated to painters. One is left with the impression that Jouet is proposing poetry as a lens, a way of seeing and framing the experience of everyday life.

Viewed in the context of contemporary French publishing, P.O.L's decision to bring out *Navet, linge, oeil-de-vieux* is a truly stunning one. It makes an important statement, moreover, both on a public stage and on a more personal one. It affirms that poetry matters to the Editions P.O.L, and that editorial policy is committed to supporting innovative poetry, even in the face of dismal market conditions. It is a rare publisher who could say as much, and back it up with hard copy. P.O.L's decision may also be seen as a clear vote of confidence in Jacques Jouet, one that celebrates Jouet's impulse to practice innovative forms and to make things new. Clearly, Jouet has taken that welcome to heart: he has published fifteen other volumes at P.O.L since *Navet* appeared, and he feels, I believe, that he has found a permanent home there. Indeed, after a recent panel appearance in which both he and his publisher took part, Jouet underscored the importance of the editorial faith which the latter invests in his authors: "Without Paul Otchakovsky-Laurens and his passion for projects that may be a little bit crazy, I would undoubtedly not have written half the books I've published at P.O.L in the last ten years."

The second exceptional gesture I would like to point out was the publication of a critical study. René Belletto is a writer who has a long history with Paul Otchakovsky-Laurens. Their first collaboration dates from Otchakovsky-Laurens's years at Flammarion, where Belletto's *Les Trâitres Mots ou Sept aventures de Thomas Nylkan* (Treacherous Words, or Seven Adventures of Thomas Nylkan) appeared in the "Textes" series in 1976. Belletto followed Otchakovsky-Laurens to Hachette in 1977, and thereafter to the Editions P.O.L. With the exception of his very first book, *Le Temps mort* (Time Out, 1974), Belletto has spent his entire career with Otchakovsky-Laurens. Like Jacques Jouet, Belletto has experimented in many different forms. Among contemporary French writers, he is perhaps most distinguished by the way that he practices both "popular" and "serious" literature, having authored examples of experimentalist fiction such as *Livre d'histoire* (History Book, 1978) and *Film noir* (1980), right alongside detective novels like *Le Revenant* (The Ghost, 1981) or thrillers such as *La Machine* (1990). Alternating between those two traditions so effortlessly, it might be remarked, Belletto's work serves to call that very opposition dramatically into question—and indeed perhaps those categories are less productive of meaning than they once were.

Even when one takes the variety of Belletto's oeuvre into account, the appearance of his *Les Grandes Espérances de Charles Dickens* (Charles Dickens's *Great Expectations*) in 1994 was an astonishing event. It is a volume of more than 650 pages, in which one novelist interrogates another, no holds barred. For inveterate readers of Belletto, the book is a feast, for as he speaks about Dickens, he inevitably speculates upon his own work in crucial, intriguing ways. Yet clearly enough, from a publisher's perspective, the decision to publish a book like this one is a wager of sorts. Belletto's study, though readable enough, is certainly no bodice-ripper, and it is difficult to imagine that its appeal to a general readership was massive, to say the least. Among the many things one might say about that editorial decision, it is legitimate to see in it yet another statement of support for literary quality, and yet another act of solidarity with an author of the sort that has distinguished the Editions P.O.L over the years. Gestures such as that help to explain the intense loyalty that many writers under the P.O.L umbrella have come to feel for Otchakovsky-Laurens himself. Belletto, for instance, is unstinting in his praise for his publisher: "Paul is Mister 100%, the only one possessing true rigor, true honesty, and true faithfulness. He's a saint wandering through our world. He's as pure as Don Quixote."

Gérard Gavarry is another writer who has been with the Editions P.O.L since the beginning, having followed Otchakovsky-Laurens there from Hachette, like Belletto. His books are polished, elaborate, and demanding texts—and none more so than *Hop là! un deux trois* (*Hoppla! 1 2 3*, 2001). That novel puts several concerns on offer. In the first instance, it studiously vexes very venerable and very new narratives, as Gavarry proposes to tell anew the Biblical tale of Ruth, in a story set in the present-day Parisian suburbs. Moreover, it is an experiment in novelistic form that puts form itself into the service of thematics. Gavarry tells his story three times over in three separate parts of his novel, each time deploying a different "code." The first part is entitled "Le cocotier" ("The Coconut Palm"), and it teems with images of tropical beaches, along with a savant vocabulary borrowed from the coconut industry. The second part is called "Le cargo" (The Cargo Ship); seascapes and nautical terms abound therein. "Le Centaure" is the name of the third part, and centaurs do indeed stride through it in various guises, conversing in a language deeply colored by ancient Greek. Lastly, *Hoppla!* attempts to reconcile two kinds of writing—experimental fiction and the *roman engagé*, or "social" novel—that have seemed to define the antipodes of the literary horizon in the last half-century or so.

From that brief description, it will be clear that Gavarry's novel is a very ambitious one, indeed just the kind of writing that P.O.L has long championed. When the level of interest that the novel elicited upon its publication proved to be disappointing, P.O.L took bold action, and that action is the third gesture that I would like to highlight here. In 2003, two years after *Hoppla!* appeared, the Editions P.O.L celebrated the house's twentieth birthday. To mark that occasion, P.O.L brought out yet another book by Gérard Gavarry, bundled it with *Hoppla!*, and sold it at the price of a single book. The former volume is entitled *Façon d'un roman, ou Comment d'après le Livre de Judith j'ai inventé une histoire de banlieue, et à l'aide du cocotier, du cargo, du Centaure, écrit trois fois Hoppla!* (Making a Novel, or, how, using the Book of Judith I invented a story of the suburbs, and with the help of the coconut tree, the cargo ship, and the Centaur, I wrote *Hoppla!* three times). In it, Gavarry comments upon *Hoppla!* in a variety of ways, calling our attention in particular to the principles, both formal and thematic, that guided the novel's composition. In the material accompanying the books, Otchakovsky-Laurens himself speaks about his impression that the novel had not received the kind of notice that it deserved, and his hope that *Façon d'un roman* might help readers to come to better terms with *Hoppla!*, in a deeper understanding of the novel's strategies. That gesture testified, in short, to an extraordinary expression of confidence on P.O.L's part, not only with regard to Gérard Gavarry, but also with regard to his readers—that is, potentially at least, with regard to *us*.

The notion that a publisher might suppose his readers to be individuals capable of sustained reflection, percipience, and original thought is a refreshing one, let us admit. We would do well not to dwell upon that notion, lest it go to our head. Yet from a purely selfish standpoint—and what other standpoint can a reader like you or me decently claim to occupy?—that in itself might persuade us that P.O.L matters.

WARREN MOTTE, 2010

JOHN O'BRIEN

A Conversation with Paul Otchakovsky-Laurens

JOHN O'BRIEN: *Why did you start P.O.L? What were you trying to do with it? You were obviously not trying to be "just another publisher," but what was your vision and intent at the start?*

PAUL OTCHAKOVSKY-LAURENS: Though I made the decision to start P.O.L quite abruptly, this decision was the end result of a slow progression. Employed at Christian Bourgois from the beginning of 1969 until the end of 1970, then at Flammarion from 1970 until 1977, and finally at Hachette from 1978 to the end of 1982, I could gradually feel my breathing space contract at the same time as my desire to publish was growing. I was no longer able to bear having to submit my literary recommendations to people whose competence and authority I didn't admire. I don't think I entered into publishing with the desire to run a business, with all the constraints that entails. I simply wanted to be free to publish the books that pleased me, disturbed me, moved me. And I finally realized that the only way to do that was precisely by becoming a real editor. Undoubtedly, I also wanted to prove that it was possible to have an editorial policy without concessions, that it wasn't necessary to publish "saleable bad books" in order to be able to publish "unsalable good books." I wanted to sell the books I found—not necessarily to find the books that would sell. It's a policy I still try to hold to today—much assisted by the "French system" in which the vast majority of new books that are published simply arrive through the mail. Outside of that, I've always endeavored to have neither a vision, nor a precise intention, for fear that these might prevent me from really seeing and welcoming what's new, work that upsets, that disrupts beliefs as much as it does people's ways of thinking, their feelings or senses. One day, at one of our first Paris Book Fairs, I pinned a sign on our stand that read: "Literature, sowing disorder everywhere order reigns . . ."

JOB: *What were the "physical" circumstances of starting P.O.L? Did you come into it with enough money for a few years? Was anyone else there at the beginning to help? What year did you start, and for how long before that were you planning on starting the press?*

PO-L: I set up P.O.L as a result of a conflict that placed me in opposition to the Hachette management, for whom I was working at the time. One day, following a difficult meeting (while I was running a relatively autonomous department, they proposed I become literary director of a subsidiary whose output I didn't like), I made my decision. That was at the beginning of September 1982: I called Charles-Henri Flammarion (the then-managing director of Flammarion) and asked him if he'd agree to help me set up a publishing house. He met me within the hour, his father (president of the board of directors) met me several days afterward, and the business was quickly settled. I had to borrow some money from my family in a very short space of time, but finally I managed it, in extremis . . . The first books appeared in March 1983. The start-up capital was the equivalent of €150,000 today, and my share was €51,000, or 34% (what we call "the blocking minority" here). I now think that, taking into account my editorial policy, that capital was insufficient . . . Very quickly I experienced great difficulties and it was necessary to recapitalize— and it wouldn't be the only time: today I hold no more than 11% of the capital (but I've never felt as independent).

JOB: *What is the "aesthetic" that guides P.O.L? Are you aware of it? Or is it reducible to "the books I like"?*

PO-L: I'm not sure of having an aesthetic as such, for the reasons I gave above. But, all the same . . . I am drawn to books that I feel represent something new; I want the books I publish, to the largest possible extent, to contain something "never heard before," "never read before," the presence of a voice unknown to me up to that point. This is not simply limited to original content; I also mean work that expresses a true, formal implementation—as we say of a musical note—of its originality . . . and without a doubt something else as well, something I have difficulty in getting across, but whose presence I come to sense (Roger Laporte would have said: "A voice of subtle silence"). It does happen that, as an ordinary reader, I like books that I wouldn't publish at P.O.L. My choices are not led, or not only led, by the pleasure of reading, but by a deeper sense, I think, something that has to do with truth, something I sense as being like truth. Very early on, in my youth, I came up against the impossibility of writing, but it wasn't a bitter realization; on the contrary, I think that that's what secretly pointed me in the direction of publishing, or, in any case, allowed me to jump at the opportunity to become involved when it presented itself. I don't publish books that I'd like to have in my library, but books that I'd like to have *written*.

JOB: *How do you manage financially? P.O.L has now been around for about as long as Dalkey, but I think we have had the advantage of grant support and donations. And I suspect that our books do about as well in the marketplace, which means "not very well." So, how sustainable is P.O.L?*

PO-L: Today and for more than five years now, after having teetered at the edge of the abyss on several occasions, P.O.L has the Gallimard group as majority shareholder. Thanks to a perfect understanding with Antoine Gallimard, its president, I run my editorial policy exactly the way I want to: when difficulties arise I can count on the support of the group, which plays the role of an understanding banker to its subsidiaries, a banker with an in-depth knowledge of the vagaries of our profession, which is no longer the case with any real banker, as we all know. For my part, I strive to distribute the risks amongst successive projects—I've learned caution. On the other hand, some authors have acquired real fame and a wide readership (Marie Darrieussecq, Emmanuel Carrère, Nicolas Fargues, Martin Winckler, and Atiq Rahimi, for example). We are now at a point, after a long period of difficulties, where we have had three successive seasons in the black, and this, added to the massive impact of Atiq Rahimi's Prix Goncourt, allows us to consider the future with a little more equanimity . . .

JOB: *How much of P.O.L is in fact Paul Otchakovsky-Laurens? What happens to the press when you are gone? So much of the press seems to be YOU, to come out of your own brain tissue. Is there a life to it beyond you, how much do you think about this, and does it matter to you?*

PO-L: Indeed, our output does reflect my choices, and my choices alone, I don't have any external readers, or interior ones moreover, and no editorial committee either—and if I have somebody else read the manuscripts, my colleagues, on some level it's in order to confirm, verify, or put my impressions to the test. After me? First of all, I don't intend on "giving up" any time soon! But as I'm well aware that I'm no more protected than anyone else from illness or accident, I have taken measures, with Antoine Gallimard's agreement, and when the time comes, someone is ready to take my place. It's a question of one person, a friend, whose curiosity, enthusiasm, and commitment I know and value. I also think that P.O.L is sufficiently healthy and has existed for long enough that a sort of literary logic has been established here, and that this logic is itself strong enough to leave a permanent imprint of its direction and to allow its perpetuation and renewal when I'm no longer around.

JOB: *Amid yet another crisis going on here at the Press, I have managed to read your responses. They are a bit disturbingly similar to what I would be saying! I will be returning to these in a roundabout way. One of the things that occurs to me is that neither of us can be entirely candid in our responses or tell all the stories that there are to tell because we are still in the middle of things and know that what we say can be taken the wrong way by a variety of people. In other words, we are not in retirement and looking backward and feeling quite free to say everything about what has happened and how it has happened. I keep dipping into James Laughlin's (founder of New Directions) memoir/autobiography and there are certain observations that he makes about his authors, and even his employees, that he could not have easily published while still running New Directions. That having been said, I will refer to a word that I used in the opening line here: crisis. One observation that I have made about myself over the years is that I get bored rather easily and so thrive on all the unexpected things that come up almost every day, as much as I may complain about them at the time. One of the attractions to publishing for me is that, even though always guided by the original principles it was begun with, Dalkey is forever in a state of flux, and I am forever having to recreate it, find new ways of doing things, and oftentimes, or usually, going against the grain of conventional thinking. Does any of what I am describing sound familiar to you? Do you keep having new ideas for how to do things, perhaps even while realizing that, if someone were to follow your thinking carefully, the new ideas would be revealed as just another form of your original ones? For me at least, much of this may come out of the humble, modest beginnings of Dalkey Archive, and I am never too far away from thinking of the press as something new and faced with enormous challenges.*

PO-L: Yes, dear John, what you're saying has a very familiar ring to it, and I agree with the idea that everything must be reinvented each day. I think that's due to the fact that we work with literature, which is a living material—at least the literature to which you and I are attached. Nothing is similar to anything else, nothing is ever the same: no two manuscripts are alike—if they're alike, there's no point. The conditions in which I practice our profession are perhaps a very little bit more comfortable than when I started out, but having said that, they haven't changed fundamentally in any way. Every book is a new challenge that demands a reassessment of everything: the sense we have of literature as the framework of the press. Every morning, on arriving at the office, I wonder what surprise the day will bring. And if there isn't one, indeed, things can become tedious quickly. That's the reason I've never, over the course of all these years, really succeeded in delegating the responsibility of opening the manuscripts that arrive in the mail. I keep this privilege, this joy of discovering the texts and their authors, for myself. In a way, it's the mail that always changes things by forcing them to evolve at the same pace as contemporary literature is evolving; it keeps the ideas and convictions alive that led me to set up the press in the first place. Then there's the reception of the books by the critics and the public, the way in which this or that creative approach ends up finding an echo: the evolution of this reception is also a source of great excitement. As for the rest, the business, the administration, I really must admit that I lack ideas (even if they do come to me from time to time!) and that I'm thankfully surrounded by competent people who make up for my deficiencies . . . Incidentally, if there's one thing I'm certain of, it's that I won't write any memoirs! I haven't read James Laughlin's and so I can't talk about them, but a constant with French editors who write such books is that their memoirs are at best deadly boring, and at worst full of concentrated bitterness. Our life is in the books we publish, don't you think? We are simply "transmitters," and we're already very lucky to deal with such remarkable works and their authors.

JOB: *Another very practical question. I know your offices quite well and love going into them. I won't try to describe them here, but I will say that I envy them, which is another way of saying how comfortable I would be working in them. There are books everywhere, and your own office is filled with manuscripts. There is a real sense of "work is being done here," rather than a sanitized corporate atmosphere. So, the question: are your current offices the same ones that you have had from the start? If not, can you say something about your previous office or offices and how you wound up in the space you now have?*

PO-L: At the very beginning when the press was set up, we started with only two rooms (quickly cluttered), just me and a single colleague. At present there are five of us here (as well as an external proofreader), so we have had to move as we expanded (twice). And we have also completely rearranged the present rooms in order to make them more functional—and more attractive. But I think that the atmosphere has always been the same. For the simple reason, it seems to me, that I couldn't envisage living in an impersonal, clinical space. It's true that as well as my "natural" tendency toward disorder, and toward the "aesthetic" pleasure I can feel organizing it, more or less, I need the physical presence of books, of manuscripts, those I publish, as well as those I don't . . . And it pleases me to have our entire operation on the premises . . . It's great when you suddenly think of this book or that author, to be able to read them immediately or, in any case, to know that they're there—it's reassuring.

JOB: *I have little idea where I am going with this question, but will be very interested in your response. Can you name the three greatest challenges that you have faced over the years in making P.O.L what it is?*

PO-L: The first challenge, really, was to find a graphic identity. I looked for several years until someone recommended a very well-known designer, Maurice Coriat, who put together our present graphic design and selected the paper that covers most of our books (initially it was an American paper, "Beckett Ridge," I believe, which was used a lot in advertising but had never been used by the French publishing industry. We have since found less costly suppliers in Europe). The perception of the press and of its output was immediately heightened by these choices, particularly in bookshops.

Another challenge was to have different authors, sometimes *very* different, coexisting at the press and yet to avoid conflicts. There have been conflicts nonetheless, recently—more personal than aesthetic—but overall I find the setup pretty satisfactory. And the press, which has been severely endangered on at least two occasions, is still standing.

When it comes to the authors, another challenge is always trying to avoid these powerful colleagues of mine coming into P.O.L to do their shopping, throwing their euros around. Without a doubt we offer writers an appropriate context for their work, we offer them a service, consideration, a closeness that the other presses can't give them: in twenty-seven years there hasn't been a single true defection, and I now have the impression that we're on a par, in this respect, with the "big players."

A fourth challenge, excuse my running over, is again to avoid having a group, any one circle of writers, take intellectual and aesthetic control of the press, become in some way "dominant," and thus reduce the press to their single aesthetic. It's very important to me that P.O.L remain as diverse and alive as is contemporary literature.

If I think about it, there have been other challenges, other crises, such as changes of stockholders and consequently of distributors, or our recapitalization problems, but as far as I'm concerned, the main ones are those I've mentioned.

JOB: *I recently gave an interview to the Los Angeles Times and was asked about my aesthetic, much the way that I asked you. And I gave a rather similar answer, that I publish what I like, though I suppose that there is an aesthetic at work somewhere, since I am forever being asked what it is. But once again I couldn't adequately answer the question except to fall back on "I publish what I like." A friend of mine took me to task about this and said that I had to support what I do by explaining what my aesthetic is. In fact, he rather hounded me about this. I finally said to him that I didn't have to explain this, that it's up to others to do that, because I do not approach a manuscript from any other perspective other than whether I like it or not. Do you think a publisher has a responsibility to explain such things?*

PO-L: No, definitely not. I don't think we have to enter into the debate. Our freedom costs us dearly (uncertainty, risk, anxiety), we certainly should not have to justify our choices on top of all that, except by pointing out the pleasure, the pride we receive in return.

JOB: *I usually say that there are only two times each year when I can take pleasure in what I do: when the fall and spring catalogs arrive. I look at them and think how envious I would be if another publisher were doing these books. But I certainly know what you mean by opening an envelope (or in recent times, getting a manuscript in an email and having it printed out to read because I cannot read on a screen, I have to have the paper in my hands) and discovering something completely unexpected, a voice I haven't heard before, or haven't heard in this way. That is a moment of delight, as is the editing, especially of the translations. I have always had an open-door policy on manuscripts, whereas many publishers in the U.S. now will only consider manuscripts submitted by agents. I prefer to deal with the authors. And I also prefer to meet authors only after I have accepted a manuscript because I know I am often influenced by the personal contact if I meet the author first. But to make this a question for you: How much do you edit manuscripts? I know this must differ from author to author, or book to book, but is it common to heavily edit a manuscript, make suggestions or require changes, and what is this process like for you? In other words, does this process create tensions between you and the authors?*

PO-L: Out of a personal conviction—slowly acquired—I rework the texts very little. An anecdote, which finds me back when I started being a "professional" reader in the '70s, working for Flammarion: Among the pile of manuscripts that came in the mail, I had noticed a text that seemed very interesting to me. It was quite a classically crafted novel, but intriguing all the same. And then, right in the middle of a major bit of plotting, one of the characters told a "funny story" that seemed never-ending to me. I gave a positive report to the editorial committee while expressing my reservations about that particular section of the book. The committee ended up deciding it was necessary to ask the author to shorten or cut that passage, a message I therefore passed on to him. But he then replied to me that he'd just been accepted at Seuil (by the great Jean Cayrol!), and without corrections. Some time later, he sent me the published book. I reread it. And I realized that the famous passage was of course the most original section of the book, that it unbalanced the novel in a good way, and introduced a kind of syncopation or lopsidedness that was one of its most original features . . . Actually, I came to distrust myself, my ideas, and the always present temptation in us, "the professionals of the profession" as Jean-Luc

Godard aptly put it, albeit referring to a different crowd, to reformat texts, to weigh and measure them and then make them conform to our expectations. Consequently, I proceed in the following manner most of the time: when I like a book enough to publish it, yet it contains moments that leave me perplexed, I sign a contract with the author and let him know my reservations. Publication not being subject to possible corrections, he is then in a much better position to evaluate the appropriateness of my suggestions, of my reservations. And we can, if necessary, work or not work on the text, there won't be tension on either of our parts (my conviction deep down is that the author is always right).

JOB: *You said that you are pleased by reviews. I have to say that I gave up a long time ago paying too much attention to reviews. Of course I prefer good reviews because they help the book. And at times I am struck by the intelligence of some reviews, when the reviewer seems to have really got at something in the book, sometimes saw things that I didn't. So, again, to make this a question: How influential are reviews in the French media? Do they sell books? Are some publications more influential than others?*

PO-L: Unfortunately, in France also, the literary press has seen a great decline in its influence over the past thirty years. All the same, a good article in *Le Monde, Libération, Le Figaro,* and a few weeklies such as *L'Express, Le Point,* or *Le Nouvel Observateur* help a book's progression a lot. If there is a concurrence of favorable opinions, this can launch a book and allow for a crossing-over to television, which remains the great prescriber, especially outside of the specifically literary programs that usually only cover books long after they've come out (and which, because it's a world where "everyone knows everyone," there can often be a whiff of the unethical about which titles they choose to champion . . .). But I must say that here we are lucky to have a national radio channel, France Culture, with excellent critics, and it plays a serious role in the promotion of the most daring books.

JOB: *How many books are you publishing each year now? Has that number grown over the years? Is there a limit that you impose upon yourself?*

PO-L: Our output hovers around forty-five titles. There was an increase at the turn of this century. This year it will be forty-seven. I don't think, with the present setup of the press, that we could go beyond fifty. It's a problem, because it's important to me on the one hand to follow our authors and to publish all of their work in its entirety, whatever the genre; on the other hand, however, I also find it essential that new authors continue to join us . . .

JOB: *If you can name one, what has been the most discouraging moment in your publishing career? Has there been a time or times when you felt as though this just isn't worth it, or that you were crazy for having ever started P.O.L?*

PO-L: I remember a day, in 1991 perhaps, when I couldn't make a payment, and, disheartened, I considered filing for bankruptcy. I really couldn't go on. At the time I had a young bookkeeper who got angry with me and said, quite emphatically, that I couldn't just give up like that. She telephoned a printer with whom we had a large bill and obtained extensions . . . I will always be grateful to her for that because I really couldn't take any more.

JOB: *Press founders are people who are driven and will do almost anything to make things work. They oftentimes have difficulty figuring out why others aren't as driven. As you know, working conditions in France vary significantly from those in the States. Employers in the States tend to frown on long vacations, and most allow two weeks of vacation per year, though that may gradually grow over years of service. France of course cherishes vacations. How do you manage to get by with employees taking five weeks of vacation from the time they start to work for you? And when they are on vacations, are they released from all their responsibilities? I know that you, like me, have a small staff and each one probably has specific duties that can't be easily covered by someone else. So, what happens when people are gone for periods of time? . . . And I realize that I am here in part talking about a clash in cultures, but also know that you and I tend to share the same views about our own vacations: time to read manuscripts and edit.*

PO-L: I will say that having always lived within this context, I don't have the impression of suffering real constraints in this regard. We organize ourselves according to the system. That said, I start from the idea that the work has to be done and, when it is done, or when it's not threatened, I am not against what I'll call flexible working hours. This only really concerns those who work with me because, like you, I am always working—but I like that, it's the life I've chosen.

JOB: *Could P.O.L be located in any other city in France than Paris? As you know, Dalkey has always been in the American Midwest, which is about 900 miles from the center of publishing, New York. In part we are here because I like the rather perverse idea of a press like Dalkey doing what we do while far removed from the world of publishing and its influences. But I also know that in many ways it would be better for the press to be in New York. So, how important is Paris to P.O.L, and why is it better than, for instance, being in a small town somewhere, such as Dalkey has been for years?*

PO-L: Sometimes I catch myself dreaming of moving P.O.L to Marseille, or Toulouse, to Montpellier perhaps: to the sun, in any case. I remember paying a visit to John Martin, the founder of Black Sparrow, in Santa Rosa or Santa Barbara, I can't remember anymore, and I thought to myself how wonderful it was: to do the job you love, to do it in that way, in those conditions (a lovely house, offices beside a pool, etc.), to do it in that setting. But I have to say that I love Paris too much, the countryside and provinces bore me quickly, so I'm very content to work here. I'm not sure that it's essential for a publishing house to be in Paris these days. The country is small, transportation is fast, and all the various regions give a lot of financial assistance to this kind of business.

JOB: *Here is a question about the future. My view is that, over the next five years or so, most books will be published electronically, especially the kinds of books that we do. If a reader wants a printed copy, he can still get one through print-on-demand, either from a press itself or through a bookstore (and I am someone who would always want a printed copy). I rather welcome this "new world" of publishing, which I think will make books more widely available and will also drastically cut down on the costs of printing and warehousing, perhaps making it possible to do more books. What are your views on electronic publishing? Is it inevitable? Do you think that P.O.L will one day be publishing most of its books electronically?*

PO-L: I am an electronic reading enthusiast, I use my "reader" a lot, but only for manuscripts: that way I can read and take notes or correct while in the metro or on the train without being weighed down with pages that fly off at the slightest jolt, in the slightest breeze. In this way, I bring dozens of texts on holiday without my bags being weighed down. I'm also in the process of digitizing my entire catalogue. However, I don't believe that electronic reading will supersede paper reading anytime soon, though it presents so many possibilities! If only the flicking through a text, hopping forward, instantly skipping back, etc. In any case I'm making it a rule never to publish solely in electronic format. I have the feeling that's an easy option, which must be avoided at all costs. It's not very rational, it's just a feeling, but it's deeply embedded in me.

JOB: *Do you have a clear or semi-clear sense of who your readers are? I am thinking of age groups in particular. Are they younger readers? Are most university-educated? Do you try to find out who they are?*

PO-L: A long way back, when I was with Hachette and running Hachette/ P.O.L, we inserted a postcard survey into the books. The readers put down their addresses and some information of a sociological nature, if they wished. One day we decided to invite those of them in the Paris region to an information and exchange meeting. Around fifty people came. It was very strange:

every class, every age was represented. There was nothing to learn from this "sample." I didn't try it again but I notice, for example at book fairs, the extreme diversity of buyers, or of the people who ask us questions or tell us about their impressions of reading our books. Of course, there is generally a rather elevated level of culture, but this seems to have been attained via very different routes, not necessarily by way of advanced university studies, for example. The taste, the passion for reading comes in such an unexpected way, sometimes very accidentally. As is written in a certain book: "The wind blows where it wills."

JOB: *Let me go back to the question of pleasure. What is it that gives you pleasure in publishing? I suppose once again I am asking you this question in the context of your having started P.O.L and that you have had to face all kinds of challenges over the years that may have had little to do with what you thought all of this would be like. Are there times or moments when you feel that it has been worth dedicating yourself to this dream of yours? What are those moments?*

PO-L: I remember that when Henri Flammarion and I signed papers setting up the company at the end of 1982, his secretary told me that he'd then gone into his office with the contract and said, "Well now he'll learn all about insomnia!" He was right. But, because of those moments you've asked about, I don't regret any of my sleepless nights. So, those moments: first and foremost the discovery of a new author, that is to say the opening of his manuscript. This manuscript arrives like all the others, its packaging differs in no way from the others, neither does its typography, but suddenly, very quickly, you know that you have something new before you, something like an apparition. There are modest apparitions, and others which are quite striking. But something begins, you feel it deep down. Then comes the first meeting with the author, and each time that verification: always, in one way or another, obvious or subtle, due to some small detail, he is like what he writes. I refuse to meet authors who have sent me their first manuscript before having read them: I only want to see the text to begin with. But the first meeting is always very moving, the author's pleasure when he learns he'll be published, which always gives you so much joy. Afterward, the books live out complicated destinies. I don't see why I should deny my pleasure: success fills me with joy, critical recognition, public success, literary prizes . . . Non-success saddens me but doesn't make me miserable . . . We carry on, that's all. Because another joy consists in seeing, following, generating the reputation of the work, whether it's recognized immediately or not. And it's a great joy to see a work settling into the body of literature, little by little, to see it taking its place there. I've been practicing this profession for forty years, directing this press for almost thirty. I've experienced that joy many times, it cannot be described . . .

Translated by Ursula Meany Scott

MARIE DARRIEUSSECQ

P.O.L: An Elegy for the Present

I remember the loose paving the first time I walked through the courtyard. From Proust to Perec, a shot of literature in the veins.

Jean-Paul Hirsch in his glassed-in office, the former concierge's lodge.

Duras and Perec, on totems, to the left and right of the front door.

I remember Paul offering a lighthouse to Corinne who was leaving to go and settle in Bretagne.

A plaster lighthouse, but really big.

Dominique Fourcade like a Cartesian diver, in the entrance hallway.

The cleaner, sporty, with his red glasses.

Whisky in the little fridge from time to time. Chocolates beside the coffee machine, or the apples that Jean-Paul Hirsch had brought. They wrinkle very quickly as it's very warm.

Antonie pregnant, Vibeke pregnant.

Thierry with a blue and white striped French sailor shirt, and blue plimsolls within arm's reach.

Frédéric Maria.

Emmanuelle Touati.

The tall piles of books wrapped in plastic, like big white Lego blocks. Then enclosed one by one in kraft paper: "publicity department."

Paul telling us how they ended up with the white, crenulated covers. There must be a specific word for this grade of paper. He told me before but I no longer remember.

I remember having suggested to Paul using recycled paper, like those responsible Canadian authors, but I can't remember his response very well. Maybe maritime pine from the Landes forest could be used, as they are for Saint Marc detergent powder? Those pines are planted, cut, replanted. All the same, it worries me.

I don't remember seeing a single live animal at P.O.L. Maybe Boudu, Marie Depussé's dog? I'm not sure.

I remember the telephone number, unchanged, a rhythm, a color: zero one four three five four two one two.

The interns. Certain names, certain faces.

Music sometimes, since people have begun listening to music on computers. I don't remember the name of the girl who was always listening to baroque music; that used to drive Jean-Paul crazy.

The Italian trattoria where we used to go and have lunch, Passage de l'Hirondelle, linked in my mind to another passage from a Patrick Modiano novel. I don't remember which one.

Croissants from Chez Paul's sometimes, the bakery next door.

I don't remember all that many things. Not much of a memory: what's current, what's modern. The taste for the present, for the books to come, the days to be lived.

The street: the students from the Fénelon lycée, the Lebanese crepe vendors, the Parisian souvenir shops, the Irish pub, the tea shop called Mariage (the name seemed very strange to me when I was younger), the cinema, the hairdressers (it seems to me that there's another one opposite). And the pink nightclub, Chuchotte's, an erotic club where Paul and Jean-Paul had said they would go "if they won the Goncourt": it's fifteen years ago I heard that. What chickens. They won it and they didn't even go.

Jean-Paul, on the telephone, it's 12:59, "We got it." The Goncourt. Me so pregnant I couldn't see my toes. The celebration, the relief (the money). Several days later, the party, three dances, two glasses of champagne, and the birth of my daughter, just when New Morning came out, whose name means what it says.

P.O.L was previously located at Villa d'Alésia, in the XIVe arrondissement. The address used to be on the first page of the books, I didn't know the place. Now I live just beside it, I pass in front of the building where P.O.L is no longer situated.

I remember Christophe Tarkos.

I remember Guillaume Dustan.

Jean-Paul Hirsch's pink Tati brand jacket the first time I saw him.

Paul's Agnès B shirts.

Paul and Jean-Paul giving up alcohol.

Paul and Jean-Paul sulking with each other.

Paul announcing to me that Gallimard is acquiring shares in the company.

Paul announcing to me that he's leaving his wife.

Jean-Paul announcing to me that he's sick. Shit.

Jean-Paul announcing to me that the results are good.

All those authors, all those egos, all those jealousies. The number of misunderstandings. The rarity of collective happiness.

Paul going through the back door with his own key.

Edouard Levé's suicide.

Paul calling me to tell me that he likes my novel, though that he's not sure, but he's never sure with first novels, that he needs time to think about it. I can see the exact place, the telephone with its twisted cord. The joy, the hope, the doubt, the beginning.

Translated by Eric Lamb

GÉRARD GAVARRY

Paul Otchakovsky-Laurens Descending a Staircase

> *I always thought that as a painter it was better to take*
> *inspiration from a writer rather than from another painter.*
> —Marcel Duchamp, interview with James Johnson Sweeney

> *This guy is completely nuts, but I think I'm going to follow him.*
> —Georges Perec, private conversation

He is upstairs in the editorial loft, forever entrenched in stacks of manuscripts while downstairs we keep watch for the moment that he will come down, anxious to join his authors, upon having at last decided to take a break from reading. Of course, a unanimous sigh of relief will accompany his appearance, resonant and sustained, or at least the beginning of such an "Ah!" because all of a sudden: the light went out! . . . went out! . . . A classic power outage could have been to blame, and considering the time and the season, the darkness would have been pitch-black and our clamor, far from being interrupted, would have been amplified immediately, its initial enthusiasm replaced by a combination of surprise, burgeoning merriment, irritation, and excitement.

But in fact things turned out differently—which is why, for the moment, we were speechless.

A switch was then accidentally flipped, or some device installed in secret deliberately turned itself on. A light emerged out of the darkness that began to flicker as it brightened, scattering sparks that, while multiplying the image of our publisher in front of our eyes, disjointed his movement down the stairs into a series of freeze frames. How many Paul Otchakovsky-Laurenses were there? Impossible to count them—which isn't to say that they were innumerable, but one was blurred, one incomplete, one of them covered by another, and that one covered by the one following him, and so on, like in Étienne-Jules Marey's famous chronophotograph, where you can see the repeated image of a hurdler and his flight path, just as repetitive, leaving a trace of four black dots and three white dots that the inventor used as reference points. The fact remains that, whether clear or not, or even partially visible, each time that he appeared, with a clarity that was in no way diminished by the brevity of the apparition, it was obviously him, it was Paul Otchakovsky-Laurens.

Following the event, the group of witnesses to this stroboscopic incident attempted to mutually convince ourselves that the event had actually happened. We talked about how long it had lasted—how many seconds? six, five, or not even five seconds? . . . And fixedness, mobility, retinal image, pause, speed, and persistence: we argued about all of that, our gazes tending to drift obliquely toward a far-off emptiness—wincing eyelids, half-open—the usual gestures that accompany an attempt to reconstruct a reliable account of a past event in the absence of any visual image.

"Ah, yes!" I exclaimed to myself.

And then once more, this time with the inner voice louder and with the *S* in "yes" more strongly stressed and prolonged:

"Ah, ye*sss*!"

The first exclamation was in response to my sudden recognition of not only the curly mop of hair belonging to one or another of the Paul Otchakovsky-Laurenses coming down the stairs, but also the recognition of the familiar angle at which he held his head—leaning gently toward the shoulder, almost tenderly, maternally—while the second exclamation was elicited by the striking, somewhat meditative manner in which this Paul Otchakovsky-Laurens covered his entire mouth, chin, and goatee with an enveloping clamp of thumb and four opposing fingers.

"That gesture, that expression," I said to myself at that moment, at the foot of the stairs leading up to the editorial loft, "That is so much like him!"

Immediately after, there was another flash of light—so soon after the previous one that the two visions I beheld actually appeared simultaneous—and with the same miniscule, intimate, and delicious shiver, I pieced together the image of his large-framed glasses under the brim of his cap, and his two long arms exposed bare and pale by his short-sleeved T-shirt. They were the same long arms that I can see in my memory of the first time that they were revealed to me, which happened to be amid a similar flood of light: turned toward the sun and willingly exposed to its brilliance, Paul Otchakovsky-Laurens sat upright on the floor in a kind of Zen monastery, leaning against a sliding screen that guarded a dark hallway. We talked film, books, and publishing. Then we remained silent for a while, tasting the surrounding calmness that was disturbed only by the hollow sound of the wooden floor pounded by the running feet of a child playing, off in the distance. Paul said that he hoped he would always remain a child, faithful and stubborn in his commitment to his whims when confronted by the condescending reasoning of adults. And with that, he leapt to his feet and began playing basketball, playing the role of both the player dribbling the ball and the coach shouting instructions: b'boom b'boom b'boom ba'boom ba'boom bounce bounce bounce / "Five!" "Play, play, play, play!"

The event in the stairwell wasn't anything like that, of course, for having reached the first or second step on his way down from the loft, another Paul Otchakovsky-Laurens appeared, this one in a fit of laughter, with his head thrown back though also hunched into his shoulders, just as I had seen him out on his terrace one day in Paris, and another time in the car on the way to Dreux, and yet another time on a vast empty beach on the Normandy coast . . . It was low tide, nighttime, during the summer. It had been really hot recently, and instead of the usual nocturnal freshness, a scalding humidity emanated from the murky vastness, completely dominating the surrounding space and thickening the amphibian air even as it passed into the lungs and stuck the clothing to one's skin. Those sensations undoubtedly threw each of us into our own experience, lived either in this place or in another, near or far. It happened in such a way that the memories that seemed so tightly melded together on that day nevertheless arose from the most varied scenes and landscapes . . . As for the Paul Otchakovsky-Laurens on the Normandy coast, which sea or delta was he thinking about? Which mangrove, or rice paddy, or jungle occupied his mind? Who, what, which voice, which language, and which method of employing or pronouncing it, which *torrential rain falling onto mountaintops*, which *water trickling down to fill the cracks of the earth*, which *wide rivers filling the oceans*? . . . And I myself—even in petto, on a Parisian balcony or in the car or on the beach, and at the foot of the editorial loft as well:

"That is so much like him!"

Many of the witnesses to the infamous descent of the staircase would question this assertion. One of them said that the strobe effect transformed the laughing figure to such a degree that for a moment he looked exactly like Édith Piaf. A second witness meditated on that image: "Édith Piaf!? . . . Mmm . . . Well, maybe. Ah, yes, I see a little Piaf . . . Yes, Piaf. I do see the resemblance." A third witness did not see, had never seen any laughing figure in the stairwell. Pronouncing the three letters *P*, *O*, *L*, with a noticeable pause between each, he proclaimed: "To me it looked more like an overworked PO-L who doesn't get enough sleep. An out-of-breath descender. He should really work out more often. Yes, he seemed tired, incapable, rooted to the spot. The dust amid the dust. He should exercise, go for a run along the river under the sun in an orange tracksuit or something . . ." And among the eruption of commentary, someone denied seeing the curly mess of hair and even the goatee altogether, while someone else disagreed with this and playfully went as far as to imagine these features reversed, the goatee on top and the mess of hair on the bottom—the palindromic head of Paul Otchakovsky-Laurens. Some other reactions: not such long and thin arms, or yes, actually they were, long skinny arms, but no way was he wearing glasses. And similar disagreements: not at all feminine, or yes feminine but not at all like Piaf—the clothes were too contemporary, the eyes too dark, the hair too thick and too dense. In any case, did Piaf ever wear her hair with such long and straight bangs as that?!

The discussion got even more lively. The witnesses unanimously agreed on some of the details. They all remembered the sputtering light and its repeated blinding effect. All of them said that they got an impression of both fixity and movement, having perceived the brevity of each image and at the same time the way in which the images persistently attacked the retina. They all felt an overload of visual stimuli, as well as a kind of fuzziness that ensued, which completely skewed their perception of space and time. Outside of these few subjects of unanimity, there was no agreement on what made or could have made Paul Otchakovsky-Laurens recognizable, or identifiable, and for that matter how he himself dealt with these difficulties in his encounters with reflective surfaces or with his shadow on the wall. Voices, questions, and assertions entered the conversation one after another, but for all their efforts, they were not able entirely to reconstruct the apparition of Paul Otchakovsky-Laurens in the doorway to the very private editorial loft, nor were they able wholly to reconstruct his descent of the staircase. He was seen wearing a suit. Seen wearing jeans. Seen wearing a tweed jacket. Seen with a cigar. Seen with or without a wool cap on his head. When he stretched his gait to reach the fourth step down from the top, he was recognizable, his massive body, his wide torso, his cheeks, as well as his avian profile. A brief glimpse of his bare chest was seen under his V-neck sweater. And his young lady's shoulder. And his shaved head, as his foot reached the fourth step from the top. His crown of graying hair was seen, and his wavy hair parted to the side, and his silky hair coming all the way down to the small of his back, and his short and frizzy hair, and his mane of blond hair. One would have seen and recognized the silhouette of a boy used to being taller than everyone. Likewise recognized, as his foot reached the fourth step from the top, was the way that he kept his eyes cast down, with his palm to his cheek, in the posture that classic painters associate with melancholy.

Faced with so many divergent images, words became so discouraging that they grew more and more scarce. Voices dwindled. The jumbled noise of muddled speech diminished to near silence, from which the only sounds to emerge were the occasional clink of bottles and the muffled sound of the communal trample of feet upon the bamboo floor matting. All around us, our books were dozing, piled on top of desks and lining the walls of the P.O.L office, while the isolated and inaccessible editorial loft, although modest in elevation, seemed like a place beyond compare. Numerous furtive glances lifted up toward it, encountered its closed door only to dart away and then back to the door again and again, to no avail. Above all things, or beings, the trajectory of those glances intersected the paths of our floating memories: an umpteenth Paul Otchakovsky-Laurens, his blue eyes deep in contemplation, yet intently focused on us, and the way in which his foot took rest on a step without putting any weight on it; or it was the memory of something that he'd said one day about feet, as a matter of fact, an anecdote that he told—his own forty-year descent of a staircase that was an altogether different sort of ordeal for his toes than the staircase leading down from the editorial loft; or the fact that a foot placed on the ground precisely covers the area upon which it marks its outline—these words, soaring freely in the air like the barber's secret that the whisper of the wind betrays, the secret that blows and murmurs everywhere to divulge the news that Midas, King Midas, has donkey ears . . . these words were recognized by us as literature itself.

But back to the flashing light. Let's not digress from that theatrical moment when the flashing light harmonized the eternal and the ephemeral. And the moment when all of the Paul Otchakovsky-Laurenses were descending the staircase . . . Have I mentioned that I found one of them in particular to be more accurate, if not to say more sympathetic, than the others—the one with the mustache? I had never met him before. I'd only seen a picture of him. He had a mustache. Hat and mustache. But upon arriving at what was our first meeting, somewhere in Paris, in the Ve arrondissement, near the Sorbonne, the hat was there but the mustache was missing! . . . Still: it was nevertheless him. He was there to give a talk at the neighboring École de Chartes, which was the occasion for our meeting. Before his talk he introduced me to a respectable woman who was curious about my work. When she asked what kind of novels I wrote, the lecturer interrupted and responded for me: "Pornography, my dear, exclusively pornography, your preferred genre." As he then turned toward me, displaying the serene expression of a man having fulfilled his responsibility with great lucidity, he nodded his head while simultaneously rapping the emptiness in front of him with his hand as if saying: "Leave it be, don't worry about it, this bitch deserves it." And without directing another word or glance toward the woman, he grabbed me by the arm and led me to the old lecture hall where an audience, "overheated by old age," as he himself put it, awaited him.

Where is he by now? How many more steps lie ahead of him before he meets us on the bamboo floor matting? And what if immobility wins out over movement, will he be trapped as a prisoner of the staircase forever, frozen in multiple poses and destined to be in transit indefinitely and never arriving? . . .

Some of my companions in waiting imagined an even worse scenario.

Let us remember Étienne-Jules Marey's hurdler, they remarked. In the blink of an eye, a viewer's impression that the figure in the image is moving forward can be replaced by the opposite notion, that the figure is in fact moving backward. Similarly, our eyes might have been taking in Paul Otchakovsky-Laurens making his way *up* the stairs, not *down*. Instead of coming closer, he is getting farther away. He might soon be at the doorway to the editorial loft, passing through it in reverse, to continue his reading undisturbed . . . Some of us could hear him from below: "*Very happy to see it* / delightful / *together a lot* / You? But you / *that's it!*" . . . And some could already imagine the cramped dimensions and the clutter of the loft, and the way its low ceiling forces one to sit hunched over. According to them, this is why Paul Otchakovsky-Laurens's posture is a little curved. This is also why he sometimes exhausts himself trying to reassemble an overturned a stack of documents, comprised of mixed-up, stray, scattered sheets of paper. For a long time he looks under the computer and under the bed with no success. He whacks his head on the ceiling as he tries to sit up, his head bounces toward the wall where a violent scrape tears his ear off, which falls to the ground. He throws his back out while trying to reach down too quickly and pick it up. He yells. He swears that he will abandon books forever.

For my part, I remain convinced that he is definitely on his way down rather than up the staircase, and that in the midst of the darkness and flashing light we will soon be raising our glasses in a toast with him. Or at most we will see him in a new light, our perceptions altered by having witnessed his multiplication. We might suspect that the numerous copies of Paul Otchakovsky-Laurens that appeared to us so vividly were only able to come into being for just that brief moment. Perhaps all are contained within the original. Or perhaps each double will remain thereafter on the staircase, but invisible, in a ghostlike state, forever lingering on whatever step—or even in the loft— where it made its appearance. In any case, Paul Otchakovsky-Laurens has now made it down to where we await him. We talk to him and listen to him, watch him drink, mingle, smile. He is considerate of everyone. But although he's made it down to us, a voice calls to us from upstairs. It is undoubtedly his voice. Sighs of approval, sighs of delight, and sighs of surprise burst from the loft, as well as shouts and complete sentences. Laughs, groans. Enchanted exclamations of "Oh my!" . . . We pretend to be deaf to these sounds. Taming our curiosity, we refrain from turning our heads toward the staircase, and we force ourselves not to look up at the ceiling.

∎

This portrait of Paul Otchakovsky-Laurens is comprised of modified quotations, some more faithful to the originals and some less, from: Georges Perec, Serge Daney, Jacques Jouet, Harry Mathews, Olivier Cadiot, Jean-Charles Massera, Marguerite Duras, Nicolas Vatimbella, Nathalie Quintane, Daniel Oster, Fred Léal, Emmanuel Hocquard, and René Belletto. It also contains virtual borrowings from or allusions to all P.O.L authors, dead, living, or yet to come. My thanks to all of them.

Translated by Eric Lamb

JACQUES JOUET

Five Books Published by Paul Otchakovsky-Laurens: A Critical Poem

I don't exclusively read books published by Paul Otchakovsky-Laurens. I don't read all the books published by Paul Otchakovsky-Laurens. That being said, I want to talk about five of them that, after I discovered them, became extremely important to me. And remain so. These five selections form a sort of personal favorites list, with all of the injustice inherent in such a list. It would not have been difficult to add five more.

This "critical poem" employs a fifth order Latin bi-square whose purpose is to bring to mind another book championed by PO-L, Georges Perec's Life A User's Manual.

I

I remember very clearly that the first time (it was in 1978, the year of its release) I held in my hands George Perec's book, *Je me souviens* (I Remember), I thought to myself that he really had guts and that his publisher was at least as crazy as he was.

I didn't immediately understand precisely what Richard Millet's *La Gloire des Pythre* (Glory of the Pythres) had stirred inside me, nor that it would have an effect on my evolution.

Where have I read, other than in Emmanuel Hocquard's *ma haie* (My Hedge), that a book of poetry is a universe "in movement"?

It is possible for reading to be a leap into the void, as I must have felt when Paul Otchakovsky-Laurens told me, without ever seeming to tell me (as he rarely does, and though it doesn't work every time), that I should read Gérard Gavarry's *Hoppla! 1 2 3*.

How can someone be jaded these days with evenemential possibility when adventure is dared by a travel book—travel that is extraordinary in its proximity—as in Jean Rolin's *La Clôture* (The Fence)?

II

I didn't immediately understand that Jean Rolin's *La Clôture* is the last book of the twentieth century, unless it is the first of the twenty-first: for that I would have had to read it again and realize that it begins on Sunday, December 31, 2000.

Where have I read that George Perec's book, *Je me souviens* wasn't really that interesting? Or perhaps that was my own personal reaction, the first time that I held it in my hands, before thinking to myself some time later that a great publisher is one that is ahead of the reading community.

It is possible for reading to be a leap into the void, which is why *La Gloire des Pythre* is one of those books that forces you to wonder if the ground underfoot is still solid enough to uphold the apathy of civilization.

How can someone be deaf at present to the beautiful image of the hedge in Emmanuel Hocquard's *ma haie*, an outline of a wall that is a dense living space, opaque and transparent, visible from both sides, but never seen from its interior, except by a sparrow or a hedgehog?

I remember very clearly that the experience of easily recognizing certain suburban sites in Gérard Gavarry's *Hoppla! 1 2 3* was at first a sort of obstacle for me since I myself was implicated in the setting and the descriptions of the characters, but that the power of fiction and the craft of distancing, as unveiled later in *Façon d'un roman* (Making a Novel), very quickly swept away that sort of scruple.

III

Where have I read, other than in Gérard Gavarry's *Hoppla! 1 2 3*, that while crime is only possible at the price of a fleeting jubilation, as echoed by the epigraph borrowed from Brecht, the weight of its consequences being only the weightier thereafter, the weight of the blade or of the sentence?

Is it possible that Jean Rolin's *La Clôture* is about a hedge in the city, a densely populated no-man's-land on the edge of the beltway, a cosmopolitan living space in which the author-character fits like a pea in a pod?

How can someone be better off at present than reading George Perec's *Je me souviens*, since memory is rendered possible neither by the will of a community nor by a communion but, to avoid resorting to "communism" again, a *communionism* (let us remember that the general title of *Je me souviens* is *Les choses communes I*), each individual outside of that unit being utterly unable to remember definitively what happened at a particular moment in time?

I remember very clearly that Richard Millet's *La Gloire des Pythre* immediately gave me the euphoric impression of clay, of a material (in the pictorial sense of the word) that is never heavy but still dense, or else a substance had been sketched by a black charcoal pencil whose substance had been dug up from and then burned in the same land that it intended to evoke.

I didn't immediately understand that if Emmanuel Hocquard's *ma haie* periodically wondered whether "everything (was) clear" in poetry, its purpose was never to be satisfied with the first stages of darkness and to always push poetry farther into the corners of the logical and practical.

IV

It is possible that Emmanuel Hocquard's *ma haie*, with its "mole" on page 216, manages to become the sort of book Francis Ponge was never able to write, that is, a police blotter of private life infinitely superior to that of a chief inspector.

How, in Gérard Gavarry's *Hoppla! 1 2 3*, can we be so firmly in the present, knowing that the author needed all those structural detours through the Bible story and the lexicon of Homeric and sub-Saharan pasts?

I remember very clearly that, during my first reading of Jean Rolin's *La Clôture*, the facts about Maréchal Ney interested me, but that it was during my second reading that I truly admired the way in which his toponymic imagination permeated his gaze, his stride, and his writing to make a battlefield (the one at Waterloo, it is said) out of the site he was considering.

I didn't immediately understand that George Perec's *Je me souviens* is only valuable because of its repeatability, which is precisely the definition of a potential book.

Where have I read other than in my reading notes penciled in on the flyleaf that Richard Millet's *La Gloire des Pythre* was an unfinished book, and that an unfinished book is not really such a bad thing? (Isn't that right, Franz Kafka?)

V

How can someone be a pessimist at present after reading Richard Millet's *La Gloire des Pythre*, where so much sweeping, plowing, and hoeing of the generations never, ever seems to sweeten the pill of the Golden Age?

I remember very clearly that the American trope at work in Emmanuel Hocquard's *ma haie* aggravated me at first, before "language investigations" convinced me of the necessity of poetry in a language, or rather, in at least two languages, if one wishes to invoke a foreign language.

I didn't immediately understand that Gérard Gavarry's *Hoppla! 1 2 3* at best "performed" the idea of incompletion, not only through the double recidivism (a term from criminology) of its narration, but also through its companion, its "how I wrote one of my books," its unexpected and reflexive sequel, *Façon d'un roman*, which I regard with the greatest admiration, because it isn't afraid to talk openly about the profession.

Where have I seen it better said than in Jean Rolin's *La Clôture* that the novel can exist without the author touching it or yielding to it, by settling for a position tangential to it?

It is possible that George Perec's *Je me souviens* is not a text but a process, and that it truly ushers in the obsolescence of postmodernity by bringing to bear the much more durable forces of potentiality.

Translated by Eric Lamb

LESLIE KAPLAN

The Early Years of P.O.L: A Story

P.O.L's early years coincide with my first years as a published author. When I finished *L'Excès-l'usine* (The Excess–The Factory) in December of 1979, I had no idea where to send it. I followed some advice from friends and I received a few negative responses, some of which were a little surprising: in the same week, two prominent publishing houses replied that my book was very interesting, truly interesting, that it was an unusual way of talking about a factory, an approach that was, *as yet, unpublished* (and that's the precise word they used, in both rejections—as they say, you can't make this up), but . . . in short, in their opinion, it would always remain that way: *as yet, unpublished.*

Another friend suggested that I send it to Paul Otchakovsky-Laurens, who at that time was directing a collection with Hachette, and I did. Nine months later he called me, it was in May of 1981, my daughter Naruna was just ten months old. I mention her because it was a time when there was a general feeling of new beginnings in the air, Mitterrand had come to power *in opposition* to Giscard, and it wasn't yet apparent that he was *in favor* of burying the May '68 movement. The air was electric.

In the meantime, I had sent the manuscript to Maurice Blanchot with a note saying that I really wanted him to read it, even if it wasn't, and certainly never would be, a published book . . . It was an "unexpected and necessary" text, he replied, his letter kept me going for months.

Paul Otchakovsky-Laurens told me that he wanted to publish it. I met him in the Hachette offices, which at that time were next to the Musée d'Art Moderne, dark wood, hallways, he and Carine Toly among the books. Carine dropped a stack of books that she was holding. Paul talked to me about my book. What struck me right away: his youth, and what I mean, I suppose, is that, firstly, he wasn't any older than me, and secondly (and more importantly), he could handle the new. For him, the only thing that counted was whether or not he liked the book, *this book here*. He didn't have any preliminary criteria, nor did he adhere to a "publishing strategy," etc. He didn't situate himself in relation to other publishers, and he didn't judge a book in relation to other books (while nonetheless possessing an extensive knowledge of contemporary literature). I think that this approach reassured me a great deal. When we had lunch together later on, I told him that I had written to Maurice Blanchot that he, Paul, wanted to publish the book, and that Blanchot had replied: "Paul Otchakovsky-Laurens loves literature."

Those are the facts about the beginning. *Les faits.*

Paul had me read other authors whom he was publishing in his Hachette/ P.O.L collection and those whom he had published when he directed a collection for Flammarion. The only one I was familiar with was Georges Perec, from *Things: A Story of the Sixties*, and also because I had recently read *Life A User's Manual*. I wasn't at all familiar with the others.

Exploration, discovery. Worlds upon worlds.

For example:

> The hills are of a blond or pink color, and between this blond and this pink some little patches of bright green

Or:

> Turning her back to the trees,
> the heavy leaves before
> the day,
> she sleeps in linen.

Or another:

> While the landscape faded as night approached, this fabric in the air no loner hinted at anything but its transparency.

Emmanuel Hocquard, from three books: *Album d'images de la Villa Harris* (Picture Album of the Harris Villa), *Une ville ou une petite île* (A City or a Small Island), and *Une journée dans le détroit* (A Day in the Strait).

And:

A tough trip. I couldn't stop looking in the rearview mirror. Each time a car passed me, or when I (rarely) passed one, I racked my brains to decide whether or not I had already seen it before. Sometimes I was sure that I had. A grueling isolation.

René Belletto, *Le Revenant* (The Ghost)

And another:

Never had she told him she loved him
knocking into trees along the way
their shadows in the bedrooms that he numbers
and during the night this murmur in her head
cries from not saying it. articulation.

Liliane Giraudon, *Je marche ou je m'endors* (I Walk or I Fall Asleep)

Take literally what you want to ravish. Balance your sentence well ("it is well balanced!"). To get around difficulty, turn to objectivity.

Jean-Jacques Viton, *Terminal, épopée* (Terminal, an Epic)

So today, July 15th, I understand that I won't see him anymore, that I will see him again, scattered (globally), his absence undying. The name Harvey exists, Harvey's image, as if, for example, I was yelling in the street, "Harvey, dinnertime!", "Come here, Harvey!"

Hubert Lucot, *Autobiogre d'A.M. 75* (Autobiogre of A.M. 75)

A very painful memory of sending off the press copies for *L'Excès-l'usine*, at Hachette, 79 Boulevard Saint-Germain, the impression of hostility, I sign books over to strangers in a tiny room, Paul unhappy with the situation, furious with Hachette, Lagardère . . . A long interview had taken place a few days before, a marvelous conversation, with Marguerite Duras at Neauphle-le-Château. Paul had conceived the idea of sending the manuscript to Duras. It was an overwhelming moment for me. Duras's generosity. Her garden. And the entire time, an incredible feeling. When I told her that I had just read Robert Antelme's *The Human Race*, which I had in fact discovered in Blanchot's *The Infinite Conversation*, she told me, "He was my husband." The way things intersect, can intersect, become related to one another: links, walkways, bridges. Liliane Giraudon and Jean-Jacques Viton's review *Banana Split* published the interview, and Michel Butel's *L'Autre journal* (The Other Newspaper) did as well, before it was republished, first in the second edition of *L'Excès-l'usine*, then in *Les Outils* (The Tools). The *Nouvel Observateur* refused it, Jean Daniel had called me to explain that he had had his plumber read it, who didn't understand a word, alas, so . . . *No comment.*

I spent the next summer finishing *Le Livre des ciels* (The Book of the Skies). During the fall: Paul calls me to say that he wants to speak with me. I meet him in a café with Carine Toly. He tells me that he has made a decision: he wants to found a publishing house, *his* publishing house. I am enthusiastic, immediately convinced. I think that I screamed for joy, or that's how it is in my memory anyway: a café bench, a hushed, smoke-filled atmosphere, and all of a sudden, laughs, shouts, hoorays. What he was going to do had nothing to do with what already existed, but at the same time, it was logical in a way. He was going to continue with exploration, discovery, and searching, which were his way of seeing literature, and he would do it now in a completely liberated way.

A seesaw, a way of rocking things, a reversal. I think that I had no idea of the material, concrete obstacles. But it was a decision, and for the moment "reality" slipped into the background (which doesn't mean that reality didn't exist): space opened up, his action was decisive, it created a new space, rearranging things, putting them into a new order.

Here, several points.

Paul always said, "The criterion for me is what I like." Whether or not someone agrees with his choice, his ethic is to stick to this principle, rigorously.

He also says, "Success is always a misunderstanding," which must not be mistaken for a cynical and bitter assertion, but rather: a book always surpasses the way it is read at a given time, the current reading, whether it is favorable or unfavorable, whether it brings success or a lack of success.

Another point, which might have been particularly noticeable during the "early years of P.O.L," but which has persevered through the years that followed because of what I think is best called Paul's "character," his eternal "youth": his interest in the new, his openness to every form of newness. His rare capacity for enthusiasm. Hence a sort of precariousness, a feeling that nothing is ever certain, that if something is tried, it might work, or then again not: a book can work or not, an idea can work or not. Hence also the doubt, not about his decisions, but about the future, a concern, but one that has a sense of certainty at its core.

There's also his baseline principle, which to me has always seemed essential: literature can write EVERYTHING, which of course does not mean that literature can *do* everything . . . This "write EVERYTHING" makes me think of what Jean-Luc Godard said about film, which can be paraphrased like so: is it about making political literature? No, absolutely not, it is about making literature politically. It also makes me think of the rallying cry of the Fiat workers during Italy's "Rampant May": "What do we want? EVERYTHING." This desire and this absence of hierarchy is clearly the mark of modernity. The context mustn't be forgotten: it was after the '70s, during the '80s, when people were trying, were able to try, to understand the '68 events differently, the jolt of it . . . I also have a memory of one of the first conversations that Paul and I had about film, it was about Godard's *Sauve qui peut (la vie)* (known in English as *Every Man for Himself* or *Slow Motion*). Both of us in love with the film. The title and the subject, the era and its dead ends, tragedies and possibilities.

So in 1983, the founding of P.O.L. And *Le Livre des ciels*, which was printed on February 2, 1983, copyright: March 1983, publisher number: 1001.

And then, during those "early years," which I associate with certain landmarks in the city, before moving to 33 Rue Saint-André-des-Arts in 1995, there were two different periods, neither of which had anything to do with Paul's publishing politics—which, I believe, never varied—but instead, were demarcated by two different offices. First was 26 Rue Jacob, from 1983 to 1986. White offices, a bright ground floor that ran parallel to an interior courtyard, and the very chic Rue Jacob, right in the middle of Saint-Germain-des-Prés.

It was open, with high ceilings, quite bare. Because of the openness and bareness I remember feeling like I was entering a new territory, a new space, a new practice, an infinite field of experimentation. For me, this was the time of my first two P.O.L books: after *Le Livre des ciels* came *Le Criminel* (The Criminal), which together with the first book, *L'Excès-l'usine*, republished by P.O.L in 1987, in my mind made up a "trilogy."

Next was number 8 Villa d'Alésia, from 1986 to 1995. A small house on a tiny street between Rue des Plantes and Rue d'Alésia, an alleyway, a bend, workshops, cobblestones, and foliage, you left Rue d'Alésia, where there were lingerie shops, clothing boutiques, you arrived at the house, you climbed a few front steps before entering. There was always this feeling of a beginning, an intensity, that was most likely heightened for me because it was during my children's childhood, I took the 38 bus toward Porte d'Orléans, it was the same bus that I would take to go to the daycare, on Rue Boulard, there was a lightness about everything, a dancing, flowing feeling. The small house full of books, piles of manuscripts everywhere, Thierry's silent presence, the coming and goings of messengers, some sort of feeling of being not settled in, of unheaviness, everyone running about, even while sitting, and lanky Paul, worried and joyful, welcoming.

During these early years, P.O.L relied heavily on the bookstores that supported its choices, those in Paris and in the provinces. That network would always remain very important in the circulation of P.O.L books.

Very, very different writers. I have always admired Paul's incredible capacity to appreciate such different styles as well as such different genres. Poetry, novels, essays, drama, Antoine Vitez's writings, film books, a book on jazz—*Thelonious Monk* by Yves Buin.

Books by Marguerite Duras, her presence.

I was reading Serge Daney, who was looking for a place to publish a new kind of journal, I talked to Paul about it, P.O.L decided to publish *Trafic*, the film review founded by Serge Daney.

Endless attempts, some social books, letters to the editor of the *Libération* newspaper—*La Vie tu parles* (Talk about Life), an essay on AIDS. Two books about famous feminists, men and women. Some foreign authors, translations of works from English, Italian, German, Polish. Experimentation, searching, the ever-present desire.

There was the "Collection," directed by Christophe Mercier, a series of very delightful little books of all colors, reprinting classic texts that had fallen into the public domain with prefaces by contemporary authors, which ended up a failure and nearly brought down the P.O.L house. And yet, the 180,000 discounted books sold immediately and the discounters were asking for more, but P.O.L was too small and couldn't handle the demand, it would have had to double its print runs and cut its cover prices in half.

From 1984 to 1991, the novels had covers illustrated in color. After Hachette and the alphabet logo, with *P*, *O*, and *L* in red and all of the other letters, numbers, and symbols in black, the P.O.L logo was designed, with the white and black circles taken from the game of *go*, a tribute to Georges Perec and the concept of infinity. At the very beginning, a flimsy and quite perishable cover. Next came the embossed white cover, with the letters of the title in blue, the letters of the author's name in beige. On the illustrated covers: clocks in every direction in front of the Saint-Lazare train station for Marie NDiaye's *Comédie classique* (1985); a sharp and ferocious boxcutter for Michel Manière's *Le Droit Chemin* (The Straight Path, 1986); a bloody sink scattered with the hairs of Emmanuel Carrère's *The Mustache* (1986); elegant drawings of old photographs for Harry Mathews's *Cigarettes* (1988); a childish landscape for Mathieu Lindon's *Prince et Léonardours* (1987); a strange mauve and brown painting, *Odysseus Before the Sirens*, for Gérard Gavarry's *Quarantaine*

(1990) . . . Three of my books had illustrated covers: *Brooklyn Bridge*, with an oppressive black and white photo of that "cathedral bridge"; *L'Épreuve du passeur* (The Proof of the Passerby), with a painting by Pablo Reinoso done especially for the cover; and *Le Silence du diable* (The Devil's Silence), with the sad and startled face of Paul Klee's *Irrung auf Grün*.

So, the work from those early years of P.O.L: a few more excerpts.

> That night I ran after you things you have to do you do quickly O
>   rose right there
> Rose O column of air the poem's structure (how to learn how to unwrite
>   and will I get better how to come closer without writing)
>   Dominique Fourcade, *Click-Rose* (1984)

> "What would you say if I shaved off my mustache?"
>   Agnès, who was on the living room couch flipping through a magazine, laughed and replied, "That might be a good idea."
>   Emmanuel Carrère, *The Mustache* (1986)

> Upon meeting her one evening in a hallway, Rose leaned toward her to kiss her. Simulating a male's voice, the child whispered in frightening slow motion: "You know the doctor? . . . Do you know that he makes dead people?"
>   Liliane Giraudon, « *La Nuit* » ("The Night," 1986)

> but between the wind and the place
> the empty porthole turns itself into day
> an obstacle the dawn hides itself in
>   Joseph Guglielmi, *Dawn* (1984)

I can't remember exactly what happened. He must have looked at me and recognized me and smiled. I shrieked no, that I didn't want to see. I started to run again, up the stairs this time. I was shrieking,

I remember that. The war emerged in my shrieks. Six years without uttering a cry. I found myself in some neighbor's apartment. They forced me to drink some rum, they poured it into my mouth. Into the shrieks.

Marguerite Duras, *The War* (1985)

Excess (lyricism and restriction), stay close to the "real" (especially latent, even harmless condensation), which no language spares. Things, leave them unnamed; receptive, don't say it, not yet, enjoy my ability, after two decades of work, to sense the existing that they imply.

Hubert Lucot, *Langst* (Languish, 1984)

JEAN OF THE EMPTY MEAT and THE MAN FROM GOLFI-ERE: We are going to the bottom. We are going to Bottom. We want to get out. The world of action is going to give birth. We aren't born.
THE MAN FROM GOLFIERE: If the World isn't out of this world, let's leave!
JEAN OF THE EMPTY MEAT: We are leaving behind all of our hats and all of our ideals and we are aspiring to the simple hole.

Valère Novarina, *Le Drame de la vie* (The Drama of Life, 1984)

What motive might inspire a thoughtful, well-read man to embark one summer evening on a large white boat and travel miles over the ocean in order to go fishing with a rod and line on a desolate shore, all alone face to face with the empty horizon?

Emmanuel Hocquard, *Aerea in the Forests of Manhattan* (1985)

skies stuck in it, dead places
crevices voids: it, the incision
waning here. Silent sexual

lips the island of skies leveled
to gray matter. The exile the suicides

> "L'Excès-l'usine—Le livre des ciels," from Michelle Grang-
> aud, *Mémento fragment* (1987)

I attempted to write, to my adoptive mother, a suicide note, that I would send shortly before taking my life, in three days, a week, a month, I didn't know, but at least it would be something done, I mean writing this letter.

Explanations, thanks, solicited forgiveness, I send you a hug and I love you, Michel.

> René Belletto, *L'Enfer* (Hell, 1986)

There's an instinctive behavior . . . that one can try to explore, that one can give back to silence. It's much more difficult, much less appropriate, to give men's behavior back to silence, because silence isn't a masculine thing. From the most ancient times, silence has been the attribute of women. So literature is women too.

> Marguerite Duras, *Practicalities* (1987)

I see something and it moves me and I put it down as I see it. In my treatment of it, I abstain from comment. Now, if I've done something that moves me—if I've portrayed the object well—somebody will come along and also be moved, and somebody else will come along and say, "What the devil is this?" And maybe they're both right.

> Charles Reznikoff (in an interview printed on the back
> cover of P.O.L's translated edition of *The Manner "Music"*)

Alex never says much when they are together. He walks slightly in front of her, with his hands in his jacket pockets. She doesn't understand why he has become so sad since she has been expecting the baby.

I would have wanted it to happen some other way, that's all.

Patrick Lapeyre, *La Lenteur de l'avenir* (The Languidness of the Future, 1987)

Hello, said the painter, I had forgotten about you.
Is it painting day?
Every day is painting day.

Bernard Noël, *Onze romans d'œil* (Eleven Novels of the Eye, 1988)

Adventure extraodinaire an extraordinary adventure
#1 I am on the verge of writing
#2 I am disposed to writing
#3 I am destined to write.
Res est difficilis dietu
The thing is difficult to write
Jamdudum
Jamdudum
Since long ago.

Olivier Cadiot, *L'Art* poetic' (1988)

The first morning from which to begin hello my beauties. One foot in front of the other in the descent from the sky bed fur my thought is in bear fur I am hot from nocturnal filth hello my beauties from which to begin.

Christian Prigent, *Commencement* (Beginning, 1989)

Tenderness inhabits every patch of air today.
The dread seems to have retreated to the immense rounded window that is at the same time a mirror and that, always a bit dirty, discovers the beauty of the park in an indecisive way.

Marie Depussé, *Dieu gît dans les details: La Borde, un asile* (God is in the Details: La Borde, a Refuge, 1993)

Defunct as an industry, cinema will once more become an artisanal art, poor or affluent, and will talk of everything that remains in shot(s) once the compressing rollers of mediated communication have gone by. Any resistance? . . . If television is a vehicle of culture, cinema transmits experience . . . If TV is our prose (and we will never talk well enough), cinema no longer stands a chance except as poetry.

> Serge Daney, *La Salaire du zappeur* (The Wages of the Zapper, 1993)

One old Russian Jew was advised to pick a truly American name, one that the immigration authorities would have no difficulty in transcribing. He asked the advice of an employee in the baggage room who suggested Rockefeller. The old Jew kept repeating "Rockefeller, Rockefeller" to be sure he'd remember. But several hours later, when the immigration officer asked him his name, he had forgotten it and answered in Yiddish, "Schon vergessen"—"I've already forgotten." And so he was registered with the American name of John Ferguson.

> Georges Perec, *Ellis Island* (1994)

And, last but not least, here is the end of Serge Daney's text, "Journal de l'an passé" ("Last Year's Diary"), published in the first issue of *Trafic*, winter 1991. It seems to harmonize perfectly with my view of "The Early Years of P.O.L" . . . and, in fact, the years that followed . . .

> November 1st. The first issue of *Trafic* is on the rails. Since you don't crack open a bottle of champagne on a ship that's sending out maydays, we will stay sober.

Translated by Eric Lamb

FRANÇOIS MATTON

Sketches

treacherous sublimation

the trivial pursued me

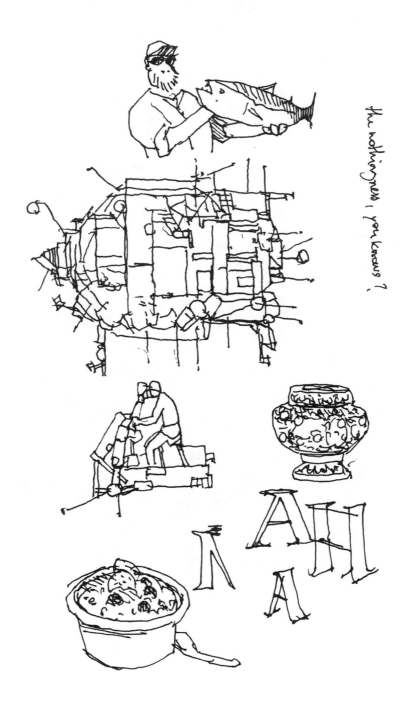

the nothingness, you know?

L searched throught the night

XABI MOLIA

On Literature as Readymade

By dint of hanging around in Parisian bookshops, of nosing out new arrivals and recognizing the same unchanging covers (Grasset's yellow, Gallimard's light beige, Stock's midnight blue, Seuil's red border, Fayard's bare and already dirty white, Minuit's turquoise on a white background, P.O.L's narrow grooves), I have ended up picturing the French publishing houses as characters with set personalities. Gallimard is the slightly uptight schoolteacher whose conversation, always courteous, surprisingly turns out to be less tedious than anticipated (as you discover that he's traveled, collects rockabilly LPs, and is able to discuss enthusiastically his progressive opinions). Seuil is the handsome old man in the crumpled suit, a polite alcoholic and disillusioned scholar, who sat in on Gilles Deleuze's seminars in his time and can theorize better than anyone about Zinedine Zidane's headbutt. Minuit is the epitome of the self-educated worker, disgruntled but sincere, uncomfortable at literary parties, which he nevertheless assiduously attends. And P.O.L, lastly, is an elegant, impassive visitor, a little too cold perhaps, who professes a total absence of doctrine but is secretly elaborating a *tractatus* of an entirely new kind.

This idea, my American friends, is perfectly false. Publishers do not exist. At least not in the way we think of them, as a kind of almost homogenous and therefore identifiable character. Publishing houses are incoherent, versatile, polygamous, opportunist creatures, in short, publishing everything and anything at all—that's how it must be, if they wish to last any length of time, and P.O.L are no different in this regard: in their catalogue, Édouard Levé's bare lists rub shoulders with Marie NDiaye's verbose phrasing (*Comédie classique*), the brisk *À quoi bon encore des poètes?* (What Good are Poets these Days?) by Christian Prigent (barely sixty pages long) leans against the monumental

Navet, linge, œil-de-vieux by Jacques Jouet (938 pages of poetry about still lifes), essential books and rare talents are mixed in with what should really be called failed novels and even some frankly sycophantic authors; and you see pornographic writers, Oulipians, masters of fantasy, Modiano clones, abstruse poets, authors of the nouveau-roman school and fundamentalists of autofiction piled on top of one another without any concern for order. What do they have in common? Not to put too fine a point on it, one would answer: that they were all desired by a single man, that they all sketch their publisher's portrait by way of his beliefs and his affinities. But I don't think that would be entirely true. P.O.L publishes everything, including the least interesting books, because it's necessary sometimes to follow fashion, to flog superfluous texts by well-established authors or to seek out scandal in order to sell copies.

But, so that nobody gets the wrong idea: the literary junk has no other purpose, in the case of the great, heroic publishers, than to finance more or less underground treasures. By publishing an Olivier Adam, a Laurent Gaudé, or a Christine Angot novel, one buys oneself the right to publish, rose in teeth, some translations from Hungarian, contemporary poets, essays on literary criticism, and second novels that nobody will buy (but that's the fate of second novels). Gallimard has always proceeded in this way, and I really believe that all or almost all of the other publishers apart from Minuit have imitated them.

Among the texts published in this manner at P.O.L, despite everything, there is one that nonetheless had a lasting effect on me: *Lâcheté d'Air France* (The Cowardice of Air France, 2002) by Mathieu Lindon, a book barely sixty-four pages long, and in a tiny format, recounting the misfortune suffered by the author in September 2001, when a bomb scare in a Parisian airport led the airline company's personnel to abandon their counters without warning and leave their unfortunate clientele in the lurch (there was of course no attack, just a lot of irritation and several hours' delay on all connections). Basically, it's a rather banal example of modern nuisance—irresponsibility, disorganization, evasive responses: the usual in a French airport, no?—that Mathieu Lindon relates without sparing us even the tiniest details, with notations as exhausting as "R. and I had arrived ahead of time, at 7:45, for the 9:25 flight

AF3354, for which check-in, due to new security restrictions, was announced as needing to be closed by 8:40." (I'm well aware that it's unfair to cherry-pick a sentence like that, but it's in order to show you, American friends, that the book's tenuous plot in no way serves as pretext for a continuous barrage of verbal innovations or that sort of brilliant digression by which authors who have carefully read their Robbe-Grillet make you feel that the subject is of little import, since *the gaze is everything*—no, Mathieu Lindon is an enraged customer and the object of *Lâcheté d'Air France* is meticulously to outline all the reasons why.)

So from where did the growing interest I had in turning the pages of this opuscule come, in the kind of landscaped, bottomless pit where the new National Library henceforth pens up its most persistent readers? Why did it hold my attention to such a degree, among the many other distinguished works available to me? Because it presents a question, in a manner both radical and provocative, which I believe is one of the founding obsessions of P.O.L: What is a literary text? Where does literature begin? What should one publish? What should one read? *Lâcheté d'Air France* is worthwhile—and Mathieu Lindon would agree with this; he who we must assume was the willing accomplice to this operation—more for the editorial gesture that brings it to our attention than for its subject, which is purely anecdotal. Or, more precisely: the anecdotal nature of this subject, along with the absence of the familiar tropes, here take on the weight of a manifesto. An open manifesto, moreover—a questioning rather than a finished aesthetic design. One certainly has the right to declare that *Lâcheté d'Air France* is of no interest. But to publish it, to display it on bookshop tables, to mention it in a critical review, and finally to read it, is to contribute to a similar form of questioning: is *that* literature then? And if it isn't, then what is literature? And where can it be found? Mathieu Lindon's book is a publishing readymade, of which Paul Otchakovsky-Laurens would be the true author.

You must understand, American friends, what kind of conditioned creatures we are, we French readers, indoctrinated by *Les Fleurs du Mal* practically from birth, then by Giraudoux's plays and Julien Gracq's *The Opposing Shore*, before being left, we Pavlovian readers, to intoxicate ourselves on Pierre Michon or Richard Millet—in any case, those who haven't succumbed by then. We admire this kind of line: "Above this earth wrapped in its dreamless slumber, the vast and astounding twinkling of the stars erupted from all directions, infuriating the hearing to the point of a compulsive refinement of its crackling of blue and dry flickers, as one turns one's ear despite oneself towards the sea sensed in the extreme distance." And, again, we drool with joy reading: "The spongy and soft dawn was pierced with overflowing ladlefuls of light, which trembled on the low clouds like a lighthouse's fumbling paintbrush." Over here, starlight has to make noise and paintbrushes have to tremble—if not, *that's not literature*. Our national taste runs to a heady, adjectival, alliterative style. We need ostentation, decoration. We celebrate literature for kings—or for bourgeois who dream of being kings.

Lâcheté d'Air France is, therefore, in this context, an insolent sort of offering, and one that disconcerted the well-raised young man I was. I found none of the usual markers of Great and True Literature in it, the kind of literature I couldn't help but love and one day imitate. Only that respectable imprimatur, P.O.L, indicated to me that *this was it*—perhaps. The opuscule threw me into a state of disquiet, out of which, what's more, I have never emerged. And if I now wished to make my praise more precise, I would simply say this: P.O.L takes it upon itself to decide what literature is. Year after year, obstinately, patiently, this publishing house has continued to welcome and promote work that tests the limits of the definition of literature and shatter the conservative or simply lazy presuppositions of our French tradition. That some imposters might have slipped into the symposium or that one might disagree with some of its loudest representatives in no way diminishes the merit of such a venture. "[W]riting is an assault on the frontiers," wrote Kafka in his *Diaries*. I would readily set this enigmatic comment, which one never quite knows what to do with, on the lintel of 33 Rue Saint-André-des-Arts. Indeed, something smacks of a military offensive in the unusual books that have been published there: an attack against whatever is certain.

D'autres vies que la mienne (Other Lives than Mine, 2009), the most recently published book by Emmanuel Carrère, possesses at its best moments a similar faculty for disorienting the reader. This powerful work, so universally praised that it will sooner or later end up being declared suspect, defies commentary by upsetting extant categories. Because, after all, what is it about? We don't really know. One struggles to find the appropriate expression. On the whole, I quite like the title of the prize that a women's magazine went and bestowed upon it: the "Emotional Novel Award." I was familiar with picaresque, comic, and bourgeois novels; with crime fiction, the novel of ideas, and science fiction; but I had never heard anyone talk about "the emotional novel." Did they create the genre entirely for *D'autres vies que la mienne*? And what's more, is it really a novel? And yet, it's certainly fair to say that emotion is at the heart of the project. The book almost inevitably brings tears to your eyes, for example when it mentions Diane, the little daughter of the dead woman (here are the very last lines of the book): "She's four years old now, and I think that she tells herself the same thing which (for other reasons) her two sisters have told themselves. Because she is the last one, because she only had her mother with her for fifteen months, because she doesn't even remember her." Together, Diane and her father watch the slide show that the mother put together before dying of cancer: "They both go down to the basement, they both take a seat in front of the computer, which he switches on. The music starts, the images unfold. Patrice looks at his wife. Diane looks at her mother. Patrice looks at Diane looking at her. She's crying, he's crying too, there is some pleasure in crying like this together, the father and his tiny little girl, but he isn't and never will be able to say to her what fathers would always like to say to their children: Never mind, it's no big deal."

In order to copy out these lines, I opened *D'autres vies que la mienne* for the first time since reading it. And I remember having asked myself, when I first reached the end, if it was a book that one would reread, a book that would age well. In that last ritual scene with the father and his child united in tears, it seems to me that it's the present indicative that makes it so poignant. Since "Everything here is true," as the jacket copy informs us, I imagine, at the moment I'm reading it, that the scene is in the process of taking place, some day this week; I think of Diane and my heart aches. In thirty years, when Diane has grown up, lived through several loves and known other heartaches, will the book's impact be as great? I don't think so; the documentary relevancy, the touching urgency will have grown more distant. But that's not important. Or rather yes, it's important, because the ephemeral nature of this work here affirms a form of greatness with which we're not very familiar: while it is common practice to say of great texts that they are timeless, *D'autres vies que la mienne* is a masterpiece for today, which can be read during a train trip, as they say of bad novels, and then vanishes, disperses into the air and thus makes it all the more inconvenient to celebrate it. Because it's also a book without any moment of brilliance, without a page you'd recite, without visible seams, a book that makes you forget its letters over and again in order better to take on its object. What is good about the book? What it tells us. What is it about it that makes it literature? I have no idea. I can't put my finger on it. Emmanuel Carrère's style is neither plain nor portentous, neither prosaic nor affected.

On leafing through *D'autres vies que la mienne*, I happen by chance on the adjective "Daedalian," and I'm initially surprised at finding it there, on page 113. I had no memory of the author using such uncommon words. But let's note how the term is used: "a huge house, Daedalian, unheatable." In the succession of adjectives, the literary substance of the second one is tightly framed, and its emphasis seemingly cancelled by the clumsiness of the third. While it's easy to point out the brilliance and uniqueness of a single phrase by Jean Echenoz or Marie NDiaye, Emmanuel Carrère's art never shows itself. And here I find once again what struck me in *Lâcheté d'Air France*: the same sense, as a reader, of a failure of the usual categories of aesthetic judgment. In this case, a certain literary mode that is conspicuous, recognizable—comforting, in a word—is again being rejected.

This is what fascinates me in the best texts published by P.O.L: a discreet and yet radical adventure in form, an experiment without /. The same is true of Leslie Kaplan's poetry in *Le Livre des ciels*, where almost every sentence is an event, and there is a torsion that distorts usage, while at the same time, everything is entirely ordinary:

I work in a factory that's too big, it should relocate soon. In the middle, the stairs. Big steps, made of cement. The banister as in school, very high.

On the floors I see the other girls.
They are young, pretty, with small, hard faces. Most of them stay together, right at the
back.

I am with the old people, at the control point. There's nothing to do, often. The old people live it up. I read.

Translated by Ursula Meany Scott

CHRISTINE MONTALBETTI

A Guided Tour of P.O.L's Editorial Offices

Getting there isn't complicated, if you're facing the Saint-Michel fountain with the river behind you (the river is very close by, a few dozen meters away; its humidity when you cross the bridge toward the Île de la Cité and then the Place du Châtelet with its two theaters and its cafes), you have to head along the right-hand side. You cross almost immediately and dive into rue Saint-André-des-Arts with its crowd heading upriver, whose tide you fight through after having passed the red awning of the sandwich shop on your right, then the tobacconist's (I sometimes stop there to buy a packet of yellow or blue American Spirits), and, on your left, the terrace of a cafe, this morning covered in a thick, translucent tarpaulin through which you must appear slightly distorted to those sitting behind it.

Next, here's a kebab shop, suggestive color photos, simultaneously bright and worn, a crêperie, a Chinese caterer, hup, watch out, you step up onto the sidewalk to get out of the way of the van coming toward you, there you go (a passing glance through the shop window at the spring rolls and beef noodle soups waiting in their bowls under films of cellophane). Now you're there on that tiny strip of pavement, tying yourself in knots so as not to bump into the passersby with your bag, you gather your coattails so as to take up the least possible amount of space dancing your way through every manner of evasive maneuver. Another crêperie, with a blue facade (opposite is a bar-restaurant where I like to have dinner, noisy and dark, but pleasant, I'm not sure why), a souvenir shop from whose hangers dangle T-shirts depicting the sights of Paris, and you almost bump into a tower of Borsalinos waiting for you to take one and try it on (on the other side of the street, the Saint-André-des-Arts cinema—art and experimental films, I recommend it); and it's there, almost opposite Chochotte (an erotic theatre with a brass sign and a red and gray fresco), just after the decorations shop: you check the white and blue plaque for confirmation, "Editions P.O.L," and you push open the heavy green carriage door with the finely wrought handle (stepping up to avoid the low crosspiece).

You're now in the cobblestone courtyard, under the archway at first, then open sky, with the trees in pots (box trees, frail olive trees, oranges perhaps, and some species whose names I don't know). You're careful not to twist your ankle on the historic, uneven ground and, at the last moment, you raise your head, which you were keeping down, your eyes fixed on the ground to avoid the little canyons running between the loose cobblestones, you raise it toward the floor-to-ceiling windows on the right, behind which you can make out Jean-Paul, to whom you wave.

But let's not get ahead of ourselves, you press the button on intercom, and at the quiet hum of the lock opening, you push open the glass door (opposite you is a staircase with a finely wrought banister whose steps have been carrying people's feet for centuries). Then you turn the handle of the little door to the right, also green, and you come across Marie and Marie.

Marie and Marie, they're the interns you might have caught a glimpse of, if you were lucky, through the frame of the window where, as in a Truffaut film, where they often appeared, at least one of them in a short dress and boots, perched on a ladder, busy shelving the books that the other was handing her in piles.

These past few weeks (reality is very resourceful), both interns have the same name. This morning, one of them is at reception, behind the desk, beside the telephone, you greet her (you can imagine the other one at the end of the hall, busy putting stamps on whatever outgoing publicity materials won't be sent out by special messenger, then putting these into the big burlap mail sack whose limp opening is far from ideal, whoops, well, there you go).

Behind Marie number one is a wall of cathedral glass whose translucent but thick panes hide Antonie from us.

She's definitely there though, in a thin, white, polo-neck sweater and gray dress, hair tied up, hand on her computer's mouse.

As she gets up to kiss you hello, your eyes sweep the wall that's papered with red, yellow, blue, and green files. You see a poster as well as loose pages tacked to the wall, covered in starry post-its whose yellow rectangular edges curl inward in the heat from the radiator. Two interior windows open high up over the angled corridor. The slender base of a halogen lamp, a printer.

Antonie Delebecque has worked full-time at P.O.L since 2003 and has become the editorial assistant. She had started by interning at P.O.L at the very start of the 2000s, in particular for the review *Trafic*. Antonie told me that she did her first publishing internship during the summer of 2000 at Balland, whose offices at the time were next door to P.O.L's: she happened to pass by to borrow the paper cutter. One thing led to another . . .

Though she likes the varied nature of her position, at the moment she's focusing her attention on the digital side of things. In particular, the P.O.L website is currently being updated . . .

Should we let her finish what she's doing?

Her little, gray, felt, man's hat must be around somewhere, so she can put it on to go and have lunch.

You leave Antonie's office and a few steps farther on—watch out for the box of books in your path—you reach Thierry's office, where he's sitting on a rotating armchair that he swivels toward the new arrival with a little squeak. Draped on the back of the armchair is his navy jacket flanked with red anchors (I've got into the habit of calling it his Captain Haddock jacket). Under the vertical light of a ceiling made of cathedral glass (the same thick panes as those separating Antonie's office from the reception), which cross, orthogonally, the mass of photons surging almost as brazenly through the window that's open onto the small back street (in the evening, you can close its iron shutter simply by pressing a button; Thierry would be delighted to show you how it works), he's working in front of his big screen doing the layout of new books.

Garamond and Plantin hold no mysteries for him, he calculates in sixteen-page signatures, will do you from twenty-eight to thirty-two lines per page.

Thierry Fourreau began working at P.O.L in 1989, and he calls himself (laughing and affecting a quavering voice) the press's oldest employee.

He gives the texts you entrust to him a readable form.

Thierry is also one of the press's authors, since in 2004 he published a story of love and grief with P.O.L: *Perfecto*.

Thank you, Thierry. The next office belongs to Vibeke.

Vibeke isn't here that day; she's accompanying Atiq Rahimi on a publicity trip to Sweden. I cast an eye over her office through the open door all the same (sorry, Vibeke), in order to be able to describe to you, well, the shelves on the left (barred by a chrome ladder), where files float, suspended from their rail, and where copies of P.O.L authors' books translated into every language are arranged, the most recent ones facing out toward the visitor with their illustrated covers and their titles that are sometimes identifiable and sometimes an absolute mystery.

On her desk, three P.O.L titles that have just been published are propped on display stands with their publicity covers wrapped around them, to the right of the back of her computer screen, huge and black against the light from the tripartite window (double windows surmounted by an upper, rectangular pane), through which can be made out, at the ground level, huge wire-covered windows and, on the second floor, an apartment with empty window boxes.

Vibeke Madsen started at P.O.L in 1998. She looks after foreign rights. Whichever author you'd like to translate, you'll have to pass through her first. You can also meet her at the Frankfurt Book Fair, and here and there when she's accompanying authors on tours. She's also the intermediary with Folio, which puts out the pocket editions of the texts first published at P.O.L. She'll send you the articles that appear about your translated books by mail, will share your delight and encourage you.

Back along the hall, there's the photocopier, the coffee machine, the fax machine, a printer, you notice a small poster of Vincent Lindon's face in Emmanuel Carrère's film, *La Moustache*, on the wall, or a telegram from Olivier Cadiot.

Before entering the next office on the left, which belongs to Paul Otchakovsky-Laurens, let's go and say hello to Jean-Paul, whom we caught sight of through the large window in the courtyard.

You carry on down the hall. You pass a Formica table to your left where a switched-off computer lies idle beside a likewise dormant telephone, which a call suddenly brings back to ringing life. Just above, left on a shelf, a dried fish that Jean-Paul brought back (I'm told) from a flea market seems the emblem of some obscure and mysterious message. You pass by other shelves, filled with the most recent P.O.L publications (ahead of you a coatrack rises up, bearing—as though arranged here entirely for decorative purposes—various gray and red fabrics), as well as the table where you would be stationed to autograph the copies of your books to be dedicated on signing days. To your right sits the postage meter, on the counter where the interns prepare the outgoing packages (but no, the second Marie isn't here).

You take a few more steps (to the left are the sinks and the bathroom should you wish to freshen up), it's on the right, the door covered with a wooden veneer (under which you'd find, no doubt, some bee's nest: the doors, in present-day renovations, still have composite souls), its handle chromium-plated—let's knock.

Jean-Paul is very happy for us to stop by. On the walls, a wedding photo, very old, a back page of a Jean-Luc Godard cover, a paragraph of Valère Novarina's, a phrase of Dominique Fourcade's, a Marie Darrieussecq text (these are handwritten and framed); an African painting given as a gift by Jacques Jouet (it depicts a field of sugar cane, I believe); the cover of *La Douleur* by

Duras, stuck onto a foam board; on the desk, along with trinkets given as gifts, such as pebbles and miniature Parisian monuments, are a series of slates knotted together (a Kounellis installation, Jean-Paul explains to me).

A miniature world.

Apparently, underneath all the files, there's a packet of stickers hanging around too, stickers in the shape of dinosaurs—its label reading *Sticker House, Made in Taiwan*—which I bought at the Natural History Museum in London and gave to Jean-Paul on the publication of my novel *L'Origine de l'homme* (The Origin of Man).

I love the view over the courtyard, the wrought iron of the balcony opposite, the geraniums in the foreground (they are very effective mosquito repellents, I take the liberty of reminding Jean-Paul).

Jean-Paul Hirsch began working at P.O.L in March 1991. His title is "sales manager," but he doesn't like either of those words. "Press attaché" would be more accurate. He's therefore in constant contact with journalists and booksellers. He speaks to them about your books over the telephone, in his office, or in a cafe, and in this way you'll sometimes bump into him with a journalist outside a cafe when you weren't expecting it.

It's also Jean-Paul who takes you in a taxi to any radio or television studios, travels with you to book fairs. Always punctual, reassuring, ready to listen. Soft voice and lovely way of speaking. And, occasionally, he takes out his digital camera to film you, collecting images that are sometimes projected for everyone to see (at P.O.L's twenty-fifth birthday party for example). At these times, you stammer a bit, you ineffectively wave your hand in front of your face, or you boldly fire a short sentence at the lens in response to a question he asks you, or regarding the situation in which you find yourself, or else about the fact that you're sorry for your terrible morning appearance, the rings under your eyes, the neon light under which you've been caught.

But then Paul Otchakovsky comes to find you and you follow him to his office.

The important thing, on entering Paul Otchakovsky-Laurens's office, is not to stumble over the small, unexpected, hidden step down—which, unlike what happened when you entered the other offices, where you stepped onto a floor level with the floor out in the hallway every time you crossed a threshold, so that, confident, good-natured, you assume you can now repeat the same movements with impunity—this step marking a very slight disparity in altitude, a subsidence underfoot; I don't know what happened with the architecture that led to this office being built just a little lower than all the others. Because, imagine it: your foot, not immediately finding the floor it expected to step onto, drops heavily, and you twist your ankle slightly, while your other foot has already started to move forward as well, so that, destabilized, you perform a live action pratfall, ker-splat, and there you are embracing, after a fashion, the ground, whose abrasive seagrass matting grazes your hands on contact; breathless and flushed, vaguely ashamed, with the wounds in the hollows of your palms tingling, the skin bristling with small, soft, translucent flakes, a little blood—very little—that starts to run (you excuse yourself to go and rinse off your hands, you know where the sinks are, you go there, clumsy and confused), no, all that is really not desirable.

But you rewind and start again, because you're not going to miss that step: with an attention that never flags—not only in the case of each new visitor, but for every single caller, visit after visit, tirelessly, and however many years you've been coming to the press—Paul Otchakovsky-Laurens will point out (or remind you of, depending on the circumstances) the existence of this step down; and not only will that little phrase, seemingly neutral, "Watch out for the step when you're coming in," certainly save you from an unpleasant experience, visit after visit, the warning will carry with it the memory of all your previous visits, humming something attentive and familiar to your ear, making one conscious of all those gentle and comforting layers of time that serve to solidify relationships.

And among all those times—now indistinct—which form the light weight of this lovely shared past, there is also the first time, of course, the initial encounter, the unforgettable, the intimidating time Paul Otchakovsky telephoned you to tell you he wanted to speak to you about your manuscript—a scene I won't go over here since I've already had the occasion to write about it in one of the *Petits déjeuners avec quelques écrivains celebres* (Breakfasts with a Few Famous Writers, 2008).

I'd give you a hundred to one (as they used to say in nineteenth-century French novels) that every P.O.L author thinks about that first time on crossing the threshold of that office again, whether consciously or otherwise. I'd give you a hundred to one that the first time is lodged there, in the recesses of the mind, stirred up by his little phrase, waiting deep below the surface, waiting, unsleeping.

Now that you've overcome the step challenge successfully, you can quickly look over the bookshelves to your left before coming to the framed photograph of Duras at Trouville (leaning on a low wall, all smiles, a penetrating and carefree black and white), surrounded by several lithographs. You note the large picture window and its double blind that falls to the floor behind the desk (computer, lamp, papers . . .); your gaze continues along over another shelf dotted with ornaments, or books standing with their covers facing out (an issue of *Trafic*, for example), then to a wall with a large print of a photograph of Edouard Levé and, in the half-oval of the light projected by the halogen lamp, several overexposed clip-frames containing drawings whose nature escapes you. Your eye, having accomplished its tour, returns to the door through which you arrived, with its little step, next to a table supporting mountains of files, manuscripts, or finished books, itself pressed up against a canvas intending something like a railway landscape, engulfed beneath a camaïeu of blues and browns.

Under this table is a wastepaper basket, if you want the inventory to be complete, and you see three armchairs (a swiveling one behind the desk, two fixed ones in front of it, black leather with chrome-plated metal bases), shall we sit for a bit? Just long enough for me to confide something to you.

Perhaps you've already felt it during this visit—that a great sensitivity reigns at P.O.L. A kind of gentleness.

Everyone is sitting at his or her desk with his or her story and personality, but all of them have this gentleness in common, very precious and very unusual.

You come to this place as you would to a house, and that's certainly the feeling those who work here have and will tell you about when you ask them— the feeling of helping, of being involved in a collective effort—and too this feeling of its being a house, a "publishing house," as they say, but here the word takes on its full meaning. Each of the people here, without conferring, will tell you that the office is their second home.

And the seagrass matting that covers the floor, the geraniums flowering in the windows, each fleetingly reinforce in your mind that feeling each of them carries within.

Which is the feeling you have also.

Because this sensitivity shown by everyone here helps each author find his or her own way.

You arrive, you say hello to everyone, you are hesitant, the stories are fermenting inside you without your being sure of the form they'll take, and this sensitivity and this gentleness allow your inventions the leisure of blossoming gently, at their own pace, as they will.

Paul Otchakovsky-Laurens founded the press in 1983, and it was located at Villa d'Alésia for a long time, in offices I never saw.

Perec is the genius loci of this publishing house, since the logo of the press is inspired by the game *go*, in tribute to he whose *Life A User's Manual* Paul Otchakovsky published in the collection he was in charge of at Hachette at the time.

Paul Otchakovsky has this gentleness and this sensitivity I was speaking of, and he shares them with every member of this press; but I must also reveal to you that there is a photograph of him with Perec in which he has Mick Jagger's smile.

Paul also often tells this story, which to some extent serves as a founding myth:

When his job was still just to read manuscripts, he had to report on a submission that seemed marvelous to him, except for a chapter that he felt needed to be cut. He conveyed this to the committee, but in the meantime the manuscript was published elsewhere. When the book came out, Paul Otchakovsky reread it, and it dawned on him that the best part of the book was the chapter he had proposed cutting out.

Thanks to this story, Paul Otchakovsky generally remains very cautious in his demands for changes, very noninterventionist. However, you can ask him to work with you on a text. You sit on these very armchairs, side by side, on this side of his desk (his own big armchair empty on the other side), and you can go through your manuscript page by page, and ask questions at the points where you're uncertain.

It's one thing I never leave without doing.

An editor is someone who justifies the hours you spend sitting down, the (considerable amount of) time you spend writing.

The most intimate, most secret, most solitary thing you do, this gesture of sitting down at a table to begin writing, which you've done since childhood and which has become utterly integral to you, your editor gives this meaning.

That's why the editor changes everything, down to the very foundations of your existence.

It's difficult to say to what degree he returns to you what you have lost.

Your hours are no longer just the frame in which you produce sentences by way of this gesture transforming experience into language, to which you have always applied yourself; they are now also turned toward the book, toward the possibility of a reader.

The worlds you invent, and the rhythm of the sentences in which you work to make them function, and where it's necessarily your own relationship to the world that you're exposing (the places you know, which also allow you to forge the ones you imagine; the people you love; everything whose slightest trace you want so badly to hold onto, and the memories of which, simultaneously powerful and subdued, you mix in with the completely metamorphosed universes where you pay them homage), your editor tells you that all this can find an echo in another being. And in this way he transforms your writing into a space for communication.

The hours that you tear from the world, the editor gives them back to the world.

What is most intimate, he knows how to make public; what is most solitary, he opens up to collectivity. And another strange thing happens too—just because you have distilled all those lonely hours writing, you begin to go on journeys that you wouldn't have gone on otherwise (invitations to book fairs, writing residencies . . .), to meet people that you wouldn't have met. So your editor is also someone who, by the single gesture of publishing you, reopens an array of possibilities, and of adventures.

Though it's hardly that writing isn't part of this world. Writing, contrary to the rumor still running around at times, has a definite place in the world. On the one hand because, during those moments you are writing, your body is interacting with the exterior world (as are your thoughts): with light, with sounds, with the objects around you, the view you have, with the temperature of the room, the sweater you did or didn't put on. And because, in the universes that you construct, that your sentences tap into, it's precisely your connection to the world which is being ceaselessly reworked. But your editor allows your writing to reach a new level of openness to the world.

And he also gives that which was purely labile or invisible a tangible trace; he transforms it into an object.

Writing is no longer the same vague moment, necessary but incomplete, that it was previously; it remains uncertain and fragile, yes, but it also becomes books, produced things, transformed time. It leaves a trace, with which you're always dissatisfied, however, and so you continue to chase after that perfect book that you'd like to write and of which every book is nothing but a very distant reflection. This distance, this remoteness from the book you'd like to have written, is painful, but also the basic principle, perhaps, behind carrying on; behind trying each time to get a little bit closer to it.

You understand then that the very singular way that Paul Otchakovsky-Laurens has of being available and of listening to you without imposing anything on you, in an attentive gesture of accompaniment, is absolutely priceless; and everyone—Antonie, Vibeke, Thierry, Jean-Paul—offers you a little of the same whenever you visit the press.

This day, when I make a tour through the offices (with, I can certainly admit to you, my little video camera in hand, in order to gather a little serious material to be able to describe everything to you), Paul Otchakovsky and I have arranged to have lunch together. I'm sick with tracheitis, and it's at the height of its powers, so we choose a quiet restaurant so that my grating wisp of a voice might actually be slightly audible.

At the end of the meal, Paul Otchakovsky points out to me that my voice has almost returned. Whether due to my exercising my vocal chords, as necessitated by our conversation, or to a natural progression toward recovery, what happens during that lunch is the perfect metaphor for what my entry into the P.O.L list represented; and, on either side of the tablecloth over which we are finishing our coffee, we mutually recall that that's just what I said in my inscription to Paul, handwritten in my first novel published with P.O.L: that he was the one who gave me my voice back.

Translated by Ursula Meany Scott

JEAN-JACQUES THOMAS

Reading P.O.L

I met Paul Otchakovsky-Laurens at the beginning of the 1970s. I had revised my thesis on Michel Leiris (*Lire Leiris*) a bit in order to publish it as a book, and I was looking for a publisher who was capable of recognizing the originality of my approach and the importance of Leiris. No book on Leiris then existed, except for a collection of articles published in serialization in *Les Lettres Nouvelles* between 1955 and 1956 by Maurice Nadeau, collected as a volume in 1963 by Julliard under the title *Michel Leiris et la quadrature du cercle* (Michel Leiris and the Squaring of the Circle). But the Michel Leiris of the '70s was neither the Michel Leiris of the '50s (*Les Temps Modernes* [Modern Times]) nor the Michel Leiris of the '60s (*L'Art Africain*).

The publishing world experienced something of a boom during the years that immediately followed 1968. For specialists in the social sciences, it was better to keep an eye on what was happening at the Editions du Seuil rather than Gallimard; the NRF was still holding on, and *Cahiers du Chemin* (Notebooks of the Path) still retained some faithful readers, but interest was shifting toward journals like *Change* and *Tel Quel* (As it Is). New journals were popping up every day, launched by people no one had ever heard of: *L'Autre Scène* (The Other Scene), *L'Ephémère* (The Ephemeral), *Cinétique* (Kinetic), etc. For a while, I even worked as a film critic as part of a cultural team directed by G.-J. S*** that had a column in a new "leftist" daily newspaper, *L'Imprévu* (The Unexpected), which was heavily influenced by the new waves of post-'68 thought. The Seuil press office, staffed by very young people, and very much in line, philosophically, with these new trends in writing, as well as the similarly minded world of pirate radio, was soon getting its new books and new authors covered on underground literary criticism talk shows that were in fierce competition with the outdated France Culture radio station. It was while listening to Radio-Cité's (95 FM) literary show *Tous avec Mallarmé!* (Everyone with Mallarmé!) that I heard about Édouard Glissant for the first time, an author who had just published a text with a new voice at Seuil, which was, in fact, a part of what would become his very successful book *Le Discours antillais* (The Antillese Discourse).

The university environment at Paris VIII Vincennes, where I taught while finishing my thesis (the contradiction is intentional—it only took me a year to go from the *T* to the *R* part in the new organization of the Department of Teaching and Research in Literary Studies, a reassignment that left me with more time for research and writing), wasn't only a constellation of the era's recognized stars, but also a breeding ground for future talents; the teaching was excellent, the research intense. In its rush to create the new academic centers destined to form the Sorbonne post-'68, the government had offered quick promotions and a fast ascent into the Parisian academy to the best provincial talents, who had always complained that under the former system, only the old-timers could hope to obtain a Parisian post—the usual capstone of a well-rounded university career. Over the course of two years, the Associate Professor positions in these new Parisian university units were being filled by the Assistant Professors of provincial universities, as well as by young, multi-diploma'd Turks from the École Normale Supérieure, who were steering away from the traditional path, which required one to start one's academic career in a provincial university. The people like myself, who had had the chance to obtain a Master's the same year the degree was first awarded, in 1969, found themselves unexpectedly qualified for certain teaching and research positions created by the '68 reform.

As I had just come back from the Ivory Coast in 1967 to finish my university studies in France, I wasn't very familiar with the Parisian intellectual world, nor, for that matter, the publishing world. Fortunately, the faculty at Paris VIII Vincennes had strong and diverse symbiotic relationships with the publishing world. Michel D*** was a powerful board member at Gallimard, and several professors, such as Henri M***, published regularly in *Les Cahiers du Chemin*. Tzvetan T***, who taught a poetry seminar as a member of the Centre National de la Recherche Scientifique, was well established with Seuil and had just founded the journal *Poétique* with Gérard G***, whose wife was the director of undergraduate studies at the Department of Literary Studies, where I taught, even though I was also enrolled in the doctoral program with the Department of Linguistics and Computer Science. Other faculty members with whom I worked every day as a Research Assistant for the preparation of a Paris VIII–Paris VII seminar on sociocritical approaches to the nineteenth century engaged in important publishing activities on a regular basis: Claude D*** worked for the Editions SEDES and the Editions Sociales, and Henri M*** had important responsibilities with Nathan. Furthermore, with the development of university research, everyone was looking to take advantage of the support of the Caisse des Lettres or the Ministry of Education to start up a new journal. D*** and G*** had just founded *Recherches*. The layouts of two reviews that would become very important and quickly gain authority in their fields were mocked-up in faculty offices open to the four winds of the university environment, the classrooms and administrative offices of the Department of Literary Studies: *Littérature*, founded in collaboration with Larousse, and *Romantisme*, the journal more or less tied to the CNRS research seminar that I was associated with, and in which I published my two first "scholarly" articles in 1973–1974.

The insider story of the heroic and pioneering years of Paris VIII Vincennes probably remains to be written, but since it is this (short) institutional story that brought about my first contact with Paul Otchakovsky-Laurens, I think that it is important to understand the networks that existed then and that might still remain unknown to those who didn't live through this exceptional moment of Parisian intellectual history right after 1968. For this was a period that saw the sudden formation of many systems, institutions, and centers of power that today, forty years after the fact, seem like natural establishments, monumental and destined to stand forever. On the flip side of all this more or less official activity, however, which affirmed the privileged relationship between the publishing world and Paris VIII Vincennes, an intellectually sound and "liberal" university, there were also ongoing intellectual/political activities that likewise implicated a large "underground" investment in the world of publishing on the university's part. The importance of Paris VIII Vincennes in the publishing of the political tracts and pamphlets that were part of everyday university life during 1969–1972 has been well documented. The university rarely shut down after the last class of the day; the photocopy machines, the mimeographs and printing presses all ran well into the night to print up the necessary political literature for the following day. Every unofficially recognized group, from the Fédération des Etudiants Révolutionnaires to the Union Nationale des Etudiants de France, to the Union des Etudiants Communistes and the Gauche Prolétarienne, was eager to protect their turf, and ultimately recognized each other's "ownership" of one office or another of a department; thus, every night, activist printing existed side by side with another type of work, just as clandestine: the work of books.

If official publishing could come up with the staff and material resources in this new kind of university, it was also because this superficial layer concealed a deeper layer of work what was much less visible, except to those who were engaged directly in it. Just as the pirate radios were set up against the institutional national radio and functioned "on the margins" in a tolerated space because of the simple fact that society hadn't yet had the time to adapt itself to the new conditions, and because the state was smart enough to understand that head-to-head combat would have been a failure from the start (the action-repression cycle had lead to uncontrollable chaos), Paris VIII Vincennes had become a center for the production of books made quickly and with limited means. The university was therefore playing fully the role of a laboratory for the future of publishing, just as the pirate radios were the laboratory for the future of radio. In revisiting this period of history, it is impossible not to note that if the people associated with the Syndicat National d'Enseignement Supérieur (National Union of University Teachers) were tied instead to the overt transformation of established publishing houses, especially those affected by the emergence of Seuil, the activity of "pirate" publishing, the '68 version of the *samizdats* at Paris VIII Vincennes was mostly the activity of the minority union of Syndicats Généraux de l'Education Nationale (General Union of National Education) representatives. It was all happening as if the new generation of university personnel that were born out of militant Christian socialism, and therefore closer to the Parti Socialiste Unifié (United Socialist Party) and ultra-left groups (the dividing line would be drawn on May 4, 1972, the day of Pierre Overney's funeral: who among the *glitterati* at Paris VIII went to follow the militant Maoist's coffin as an act of defiance both to the Gaullist power and the official Communist Party that was omnipresent in the post-'68 French university) were rediscovering the underground work of the first Christians who, under persecution, copied forbidden religious texts and distributed them to believers. Thereby (perennially poor) university students were able to find affordably priced pirate editions of the expensive books that were required for their studies. Also published under the table were certain texts that the commercial publishers didn't want to publish because they only interested a limited number of readers; certain foreign texts that were fundamental in the new areas of studies that were being founded (sociology, linguistics, psychoanalysis, etc.) were quickly translated and published. To some extent, all of these new publications opened up the publishing market and put an end to a kind of intellectual isolation of French academia by making "foreign" texts available to students in subject areas recently added to the list of university disciplines following May '68. This is how I was able to read "Poetry of Grammar and Grammar of Poetry" by Jakobson, the essential Freudian texts which included his preface to Fyodor Dostoyevsky's biography that was written by Dostoyevsky's spouse, a text that is fundamental in understanding the use of Freudianism in literary criticism and which is unfortunately still unknown to a lot of critics. Likewise, I think that before the official printing of Lacan's *Seminar*, a large portion of underground publishing work already existed, centered around Paris VIII Vincennes: timely transcriptions of the seminar.

What about P.O.L, you may ask? Precisely, I'm getting there. Humor, originality, and creativity were not lacking at Paris VIII Vincennes. It is of no surprise that as a consequence many of those who were involved in this underground publishing venture by virtue of their passion for books, and who, most likely, already had an industrial mentality even in the underground realm, in subsequent years attained high levels of responsibility in the official French publishing world. During the years '69–'72 the diverse and scattered initiatives at getting a publishing clandestine house up and running came together under a common name: "P.V." It was most likely a simple recognition of the origin: "Paris Vincennes." But it is also possible to suggest that the acronym had something to do with the norms of the era and of modernity that were fond of polysemy, paronomasia and word play. In the Paris VIII Vincennes university community post-'68, the traditional enemies were the "cops," whose basic instrument of repression was the "pv" (verbal process, "ticket," or *procès-verbal* in French); of course the "cops" were technically not allowed to set foot on the campus grounds of Paris VIII Vincennes, but they still lurked about . . . And their prey was an easy catch: when Paris VIII Vincennes was built, hastily and with modular designs during the summer of '69 on an old decommissioned military training field (that did not come without complaint) in the middle of the Vincennes forest, no thought had been given to plan for the massive parking space needed for students' and teachers' cars except for a small square meadow (probably because the authorities reasoned that the [in]frequent buses that ran between the castle of Vincennes and the university would satisfy the transportation needs of students who, as is known, are poor and don't have a car). The result: a makeshift parking lot in the Vincennes forest surrounding the university was quickly inundated by "procès-verbal" in the form of parking tickets issued by the local police. We all came to know this because the "experimental university" was isolated in the middle of the forest and was inaccessible on foot. This explanation is all well and good, but a serious reader can't ignore the fact that in French "pv" is written without punctuation, whereas "P.V." takes on periods. Herein lies the great ingenuity of P.V. as the name of an underground press. A linguistic and stylistic innovation is at work in the addition of those periods, because the addition is proof of an intentional creation of a sort of "microstructural diction device" (between paronomasia, word play, relocation and similitude, if not contamination). Another ritual that metered the rhythm of everyday life at Paris VIII Vincennes was the urgent call on the "G.A." (or "General Assembly") for an important piece of news or an immediate decision about the continuation or discontinuation of classes. Once the "General Assembly" had voted on decisions (by raised hands), the results had to be communicated immediately to the students and staff (especially in a university like Vincennes in which a large part of the student population had a job in addition to their studies). One of the documents that was the most widely printed by the not-so-clandestine university presses and left in the hands of "student representatives" was therefore the "G.A. pv" (Minutes of the General Assembly). Sometimes as often as three times a day! The urgent printing of a "G.A. pv" was thereby (always) the most common excuse to justify the use of university printing materials and machinery during the oddest of hours. The explanation for the acrobatic and nocturnal use of printing equipment "I'm preparing a G.A. pv" probably evolved quickly thereafter into "I'm preparing a pv," as a result of contamination and the progressive disappearance of the noble "G.A." component of the term. Linguists who try to explain the disappearance of the "ne" and the substitution of the lone "pas" ("j'veux pas!") amply understand language's tendency toward efficiency. It turned out that this very simple expression became a term that was good enough to use as a cover-up for all underground printing activity, since all production was becoming a "P.V." publication. The term isn't a simple abbreviation or aggregate of initials, for a creative force can be recognized in the addition of the periods after the "P." and the "V." In an environment in which the political parties read "PCF," "PSU," "RPR," and the labor unions "SNEsup," "CGT," "SGEN," and the military-capitalist complex "IBM," "ITT," "ATT," and the political figures were "JJSS," "CDG," etc., the addition of the periods in "P.V.," following the model of the quotidian "G.A.," put in place a novel universe of symbolism that continues to hold its own today.

For a long time I wondered if the inclusion of the periods in the P.O.L trade mark was inspired by the innovation introduced in 1971 by P.V.; perhaps a sort of (secret, distant?) affiliation with this prototype institution of modern French publishing, established by a self-distancing from well-established and prominent publishing houses. Surely, the independent publishing house P.O.L was founded in 1983, but the "P.O.L" sequence appeared precisely the same year as P.V. and the clandestine nature left room for the official PUV that, by deleting the periods, reverts to a banal uselessness common of other university presses (PUL, PUPS, PUN, PUAM, PUNM, etc.). Furthermore, Paul Otchakovsky-Laurens (PO-L) had in some way already marked his territory and his distinctiveness, because in 1977 Hachette placed him in charge of a publishing department, thanks to his success with *Life A User's Manual* by Georges Perec, which quickly became a separate collection under the "Hachette/P.O.L" imprint. And considering that P.V.'s existence was known by the end of 1971, there were therefore only six years that it had been producing in the underground Parisian publishing world, and some of its publications in the field of psychoanalysis were circulating extensively in the small Parisian avant-garde community.

As I pointed out at the beginning of this essay which quickly turned to a consideration of two periods (ha-ha) in the P.O.L logo, it was during this period of creation, innovation, dreams and profound change in the Parisian publishing environment that I met PO-L. In 1972 I had given the manuscript of my book, *Lire Leiris*, to the members of my thesis committee, as well as to friends and colleagues, requesting that they suggest an editor who might take an interest in a study on poetics by an author who wasn't yet well-known. Four obvious solutions came to light. Jacques Derrida (whom I had met at one of his early lectures in Arras in 1968 while he was still an Assistant Professor at the École Normale Supérieure) had just founded Editions Galilée and while it wasn't "Derridean" (a term that didn't exist at the time), my book offered a number of commentaries on some of Derrida's texts, and acknowledged his ideas on language; in the end, the publishing house's readers found that the text didn't manifest enough of a faithful affiliation with Derrida's thought, and that of *Tel Quel,* and so the manuscript was rejected. The Editions SEDES agreed to take it in principle, but they had a backlog, and since Leiris wasn't on the syllabus of any examinations, the project didn't have much priority. The other suggestion was to go see the young director of the "Textes" collection at Flammarion, of whom everyone seemed to have an excellent opinion and who, so they said, had a bright future ahead of him because he was a "discoverer." Given the large amount of information available at Paris VIII Vincennes about the Parisian publishing world and the general climate of "novelty" and "modernity" necessary to stay directly in tune with the current trends of the intellectual community, the recommendation wasn't without weight. On my own, I would have never gone to Flammarion, which at the time seemed to me like a publisher of classic texts. Pummeled by recommendations, I was prompted to send my manuscript to PO-L, and a few weeks later I received a note inviting me to Flammarion, on its dark and narrow Ecole de Médecine street. I don't remember seeing his office, and I suspect that we met each other in one of the waiting rooms on the ground floor. I had the pleasure of remarking his youth and his openness, and that he had given my text a thorough reading. While listening to him, I got the feeling that he understood its general angles of development, which he could place in the context of contemporary critical principles. Clearly he possessed a critical enthusiasm, a true passion for the literary artifact and an interest that I judged as authentic, in me as an author and in my personal and intellectual itinerary. He also showed me the flaws of my writing "tics" and offered me some very useful advice on how to "improve" my text ("Look here: forget the work on the thesis and write a book that can do without fifteen footnotes on every page to justify it!") and adapt it to the norms of commercial production. He never told me that he was going to accept the manuscript, nor reject it, he simply told me to reflect on what he had just told me, that it was a pleasure to meet and chat with me, and that he hoped to see me soon. I guess it was a standard interview with a young unknown author whose dignity you want to be courteous of, and whose work may or may not turn into something worthwhile.

I never saw PO-L again, but I well remember the person that I met and the conversation that we had. And even after numerous publications, many work meetings with publishers and collection directors, on both sides of the Atlantic, that meeting, at the beginning of my career, has remained fixed in my memory as an excellent contact experience with the Parisian publishing world. Finally, two or three months after my visit to Flammarion, I learned that my department chair wanted me to participate in an exchange with an "Anglo-Saxon" university (Canada or the United States) and that there was also a possibility for me to participate in a year-long exchange with the Freie Universität of Berlin. After a couple of weeks of consultation, my fellow graduate student Régine Robin was sent to the University of Toronto, because she specialized in Zola and Toronto had a research center dedicated to that author. I was sent to the University of Michigan at Ann Arbor because technically I was in linguistics (a "linguist on loan to the literary arts") and Ann Arbor had a large laboratory of Pike's tagmemics as well as a center on French as a second language where cutting-edge work was being done in collaboration with Bernard Q*** at the Saint-Cloud Ecole Normale Supérieure and Jean P*** at Besançon. Once the decision was made to teach and do research in the United States, there was a time crunch, and I needed to wrap up my book project. And so only the fourth solution was left: publish with P.V. I confided my concerns to one of my contacts at P.V. who knew of the department's decision to send me on a faculty and research exchange to an American university in order to maintain the international prestige of Paris VIII Vincennes, and he immediately put the typesetters of the P.V. to a Stakhanovist work pace, and my text was immediately published and registered with the Bibliothèque Nationale copyright office a week or two before my departure for the United States in September of 1972 (but without an ISBN, a norm that wasn't required at the time).

Ever since my meeting with PO-L, I have greatly respected what he has accomplished in French publishing and the quality of texts that he has decided to publish. In light of what I experienced with him, I imagine him forever fascinated in meetings with young (and less young) authors, providing suggestions to them in order to produce the book that will be a success in the bookstore and/or a critical success. Sometimes I regret having had to accelerate the publication of my first book in order to move on to the next stage in my career, and I imagine that, had I had the time to take to rethink my text in terms of what PO-L had suggested, my book *Lire Leiris* would have enjoyed a wider circulation and would have a similar reputation now as my special issue on Leiris in the American journal *SubStance*, a 1975 publication in English based on a long chapter from my original French text of 1972.

My confidence in P.O.L publications is such that when I spend time in France, I often make a stop at the Tschann bookstore on Boulevard Montparnasse and simply buy the latest P.O.L publications. This is how, last August, before my return to New York, in addition to the Pierre Alferi texts that I work on, I bought *La Poétesse (Homobiographie)* (The Poetess [Homobiography]) by Liliane Giraudon, whom I also met there a long time ago when Michel Pierssens and Sydney Lévy were putting together the fifth and sixth issues of *SubStance* (1973), dedicated to contemporary French poetry. Likewise, I picked up *Hammurabi* by Frédéric Boyer, a short, simple work in the same category as *Des choses idiotes et douces* (Sweet and Foolish Things—winner of the Prix du Livre Inter), which merits a slow reading because it contains all of the profound wisdom of the world since Hammurabi, the ruler of Babylon in 3757 BC, up to the soldier from Oklahoma City, dead in his M2 Bradley on the plains of Babylon. It evokes the old, silent, and indifferent knowledge of stones, even the ones in our museums that are there, so they say, to teach us something; actually, might this Boyer have something to do with Philippe Boyer from Groupe Change, the author of *Non-Lieu* (Non-Place), and he too a collaborator of issues 5/6 of *SubStance*? Or is it just homonymy? I also bought and read *Taudis-Autels* (Pigsties-Altars) by Marc Cholodenko; someone told me that Cholodenko is one of PO-L's favorite authors, since their first meeting when PO-L was a reader with Christian Bourgois; and he published Cholodenko as soon as Hachette/P.O.L was founded. A work of bipolar writing (I like / I don't like) constructed according to a clinical scientific alphabetical progression ("soul," "sour," "suit," "tremor," etc.). But sometimes tricks of discourse hide the for and the against: for ecologists I suggest "Pigsty-Altar of the Forest," for existentialists "Pigsty-Altar of Suicide," and for serious people "Pigsty-Altar of Order." Often people who aren't up to date with contemporary French fiction think that Cholodenko is an Oulipian author because he writes under what appears to be a constraint; read *Taudis-Autels*, that should clear up any misunderstanding. Finally, to come back to what lead to my first meeting with PO-L, I bought Charles Juliet's *L'Opulence de la nuit* (The Opulence of Night). A work that isn't from 2009 (2006), but that I hadn't read. Charles Juliet was a friend of Leiris, and one of his most perceptive readers. In 1974, when I was putting together the special issue of *SubStance* that is dedicated to him, Leiris (who had praised my *Lire Leiris* and whom a previous private agreement with the journal *L'Arc* prevented from collaborating on the special issue that I was preparing) suggested that I get in contact with Pierre Chapuis and Charles Juliet, whose work he liked. The collaboration with Charles Juliet didn't work out, but I always appreciated his work on Leiris and, as if accidentally, his other texts. In this case, it so happens that I admire PO-L's difficult vocation for contemporary French poetry. The poetry that he publishes doesn't conform to the doctrine of a particular school, nor to a publishing line, but preserves personal poetry (in the positive sense of the term). From that point of view, Juliet and Giraudon are lucky to be housed by P.O.L, and French publishing is lucky to have a publisher who protects poetry and understands the richness of its contemporary production. These books exist and offer a reward to readers who do not expect the expected. It is, I believe, without the help of the Centre National des Lettres that Juliet's text was published, and yet this extraordinary simple phrase can be found therein: "He wrote to console / the child that lived within him." It isn't about reproducing the common style. It isn't about inscribing oneself in the style *du jour*, closely following the road that leads to the contemporary

Parnassus, but rather to blaze a trail, to bring together a reading community with an active curiosity, open to the new.

Like me, read P.O.L, all of P.O.L, but especially the works of poetry. You won't regret it.

Translated by Eric Lamb

Selections from the P.O.L list

I didn't find it easy to choose excerpts from among the nearly one thousand books I've published over the past twenty-six years. I think that each of the works from which an excerpt is presented here in English translation represents other books, and each author other authors. In any case, it was in this spirit that I proceeded.

Though it might seem a strange way of thanking them, I have deliberately excluded the writers who are already contributing to this issue of the *Review of Contemporary Fiction*. But I feared redundancy, and making them seem part of some exclusive circle—I think they'll understand. I have also left out those authors who have recently been translated in the U.S., or who will be soon— notably with Dalkey Archive Press, by John O'Brien, to whom I am grateful.

PAUL OTCHAKOVSKY-LAURENS
Translated by Ursula Meany Scott

PIERRE ALFERI

from *Les Jumelles* (The Binoculars, 2009)

On Thursday, the ninth of April, two thousand and nine, at around seven thirty in the evening, Horacio Picq left the reading room in Fort Tremor (Côtes-d'Armor), located fifty feet below the ground at the level known as the "Oubliettes," with the firm intention of catching the eight o'clock train to the capital. The temperature of the crypt—which was long and humid like the intestine of a Leviathan—was no more than sixty degrees; he was in a hurry to get into the overheated tube of the Guingamp-Paris train to doze off for a few hours, his cheek resting on the leatherette of his headrest, satisfied with the feeling of having accomplished something.

He imagined with pleasure the sight of the suburbs, reduced to ever-denser constellations of lampposts, the horizontal rain of lights on the highway, then the nebulous signs that the taxi would fly past on its way from the Gare Montparnasse to his garret in the northern suburbs. Embraced by the masses of people slumbering under all those speckles of light, he would soon return to real life—the life of the city. But as he emerged from the granite steps by a trapdoor into the courtyard, he had to shut his eyes tightly, having been struck with a hint of vertigo. A sudden storm had completely covered the ground with snow, as well as the sloped rooftops of a building that looked as if it belonged either to a monastery or to a military complex. Against the somber sky in which a few stars could already be seen twinkling, the ground appeared almost phosphorescent.

The silence was broken only by the whistling of an icy wind and a few cracking sounds in the distance: screech ... scratch. Picq's first thought was of the fort's cook, whose skills had been praised by the tour guide who had picked him up from the train station. It sounded as if she were breaking endives across her knee. Did she go so far as to harvest them herself in the underground maze below, an environment that would have been just as apt for the growing of asparagus, salsify, Paris mushrooms, or any other albino vegetable? Walking toward the drawbridge, he considered that the unexpected snow was winter's way of bidding him farewell, and he knew he would have no regrets leaving this cursed microclimate behind. At the other end of the courtyard, he noticed the silhouette of the tour guide. He realized then that it must have been the guide's footsteps in the snow that made the sound he had associated with endives being broken over someone's knee. Now that he could see the footprints in the crunching surface, they looked like holes punched into polystyrene.

As soon as their paths crossed, the young man announced with a grave look that the suddenness of the snowfall had set off a city-wide emergency plan named after some warm color, and that the first measure of this plan was the prohibition of all motor-vehicle circulation, whether by car or by train. And, indeed, the salting of the traversable roads would begin tomorrow at dawn, at the earliest. Picq had neither the inspiration nor the nerve to pretend that his pressing need to leave the premises should be considered as an exception to this rule. With apparent good grace, he accepted the invitation to spend the night in a guest room.

Translated by Gregory Flanders

RENÉ BELLETTO

from *Créature* (2000)

Michel parked his car on the other side of the boulevard, as was his habit, and crossed over, in this way passing the "frontier" (that's the word his neighbor, the oculist from the first floor, used) between the XVIIIe and the IXe arrondissements. He was surprised by the great silence. The late hour, a freak of traffic circulation, there was nobody around, the boulevard was deserted. Surely it had only started a short time ago, and surely it wouldn't last very long; still, Michel didn't see anyone while he was crossing.

What silence!

He didn't even hear, as was sometimes the case, the tinkling of the keys to his apartment in his pocket.

He couldn't wait to lie down on his couch. He was going to smoke, listen to some music on his new speakers, skim through the notes he'd taken down in his notebook with its black and white cover—perhaps add a kind of epilogue at the end—while waiting for Estella's call.

He was in front of the door to his building. The words "the late hour" had remained in his mind. He associated them with the idea of a watch, thought of his watch—and suddenly became conscious of a strange sensation on his left wrist—he was alarmed, looked down . . .

His watch had disappeared.

It must have come undone and fallen off.

But he didn't worry for more than a few seconds, because he remembered having checked the time before parking. So his lovely watch was either back in his car or somewhere on the path between his car and the building. The most surprising thing was its coming undone like that. Surprising, but not impossible, he said to himself: a bump, combined with a slightly unusual turn of his wrist . . . No, it wasn't completely impossible. Whatever had happened, the watch was definitely somewhere between where he was standing and his car.

So he prepared to cross the boulevard again, sure of finding it, with, however, the degree of uncertainty common to all mortals.

Translated by Ursula Meany Scott

FRÉDÉRIC BOYER

from *Vaches* (Cows, 2008)

For a long time, the cows marched in the night of Leiden alongside Descartes, who moved like a man who walks alone and in the darkness, resolved to keep a slow pace.

And we threw the cows into the night as if fanaticism had never left our hearts.

A cow has immense eyes, black and empty. When you see a cow for the first time, you see nothing but its eyes. But those who have never looked into a cow's eyes with their own are not like us.

The body of the animal at Creation. The animal of the void. The cow.

The day when cows no longer walk the earth will be a day of obscure terror for those of us who survive them.

We have irremediably forgotten the reason why cows were able to remember better than any other animal what were once the sun and the water, women and children, fruits and vegetables. Cows are full of ancient, chewed-over memories. Their one invincible and irresistible desire is to perpetuate themselves forever. They are full of innumerable promises, they are full of young cows. It was the obscene gentleness, the overt impassibility of cows that pierced our minds. We had no love for them. We feared the cows. They fattened themselves peacefully. They ate slowly. They shat green, tender cow pies.

Translated by Gregory Flanders

OLIVIER CADIOT

from *Retour définitif et durable de l'être aimé*
(The Definitive and Lasting Return of the Loved One, 2002)

I'm swimming, my head breaks the mirror of the water, the rest of my body remains submerged, I break through its surface, powder of larva, black mirror, I am larger than before.

I'm swimming.

I am the water, I am a whole, I am not afraid, it's over, I'm coming back, I am here, dust of nymphs, flowers of hedges, ashen film of tiny dead insects abandoned to the current, I sing, so small against the white upside-down sky, arms crossed, then uncrossed, a motor.

I'm swimming.

It's me, I can speak, summarized ideas, simple images, tangled thoughts, a dozen tiny trees, here is my forest, four leaves this year, eight next year, that will be fine, I break down my gestures in the elasticity of the black reservoir, a breaststroke between the hedges, this is my body, this is me, doing the frog, I build up, I break down, I advance.

I'm swimming.

I come back up, past days return, it's already morning, migration from beneath, I steer myself, I come back, hello it's me, your friend, fins far away, off under the water, yellow catfish body, fountain nymph, colored in the green mass of moss from the wells, hair of grass.

Idling in the slow current.

The dull sound of letters slowed by water, I move my arms, I widen my eyes to say Hurry, I articulate, vowel, consonant, vowel, no response.

He doesn't understand.

So I am someone who speaks to another person who wouldn't recognize me, is that it? Quick hand movement above my head to say Hello, finger pointed to my chest to say It's me, no, too far, too much wind, separated by a lagoon of sorts that cuts the beach in two, small robe, light wind, morning, but we danced together, yes, yes, it's me, I cry out his name through my hands at my face.

Nothing.

He hears nothing, forgive me, movement of hands raised to each side, slowly, to say I'm sorry, I don't recognize you at all.

Bubbles.

I swim against the current between the water lilies whose stems are exactly as deep as the water, underwater breaststroke, head breaking the mirror, ashen film, dead insects, bits of leaves, powder of tiny bodies, I have absolutely no fear, my head is in rhythm with the passing landscape, window to a cloudy sky, the weather is beautiful, the light is true, I hum between the undulating reeds, hello it's me, I'm singing: come into the gentle water, dolce vita, vita nova, it's me, coda, come on, then another one: I compose, I build myself up, I break myself down, pause, this is for you.

I'm swimming.

Message, I move my arms, I make letters at the speed of sound with my body, stop, it's me, light years later, quick, dive in here, come, don't be afraid, hurry, it's urgent, under the water, come on, jump in.

Now.

Translated by Gregory Flanders

RENAUD CAMUS

from *Loin* (Far Away, 2009)

We must look at everything, and read everything, as if it was for the last time. We shouldn't tell ourselves that we have time, because we don't. If by some extraordinary chance we weren't the ones who were going to die, it would be that woman met one time who would disappear without a trace, or that village which would be joined up to the suburbs and swallowed by them, that language which would soon no longer be understood by anyone, those lines that would never again take on the wit and singularity they'd assumed at first glance. And Jean found so much power and such value in this conviction he'd developed— that we should look at things, and beings, and sentences, and places, with the thought that our eyes would never fall on them again; that we'll never again see that face or that paragraph, since either we or they or it would be erased before there was any chance of another encounter—that he was struggling constantly to behave as though this was indeed the case. Although, quite often, perhaps even *more often than not*, the opposite was far more likely: repetition, seeing the same people and things over and again, only experiencing life, only feeling it, on a superficial level. Nonetheless, this severing of himself from familiar things had become something like a powerful drug to him, throwing him into a state of such elation, into such a vibrant serenity, so precious now in his eyes, that every time he arrived somewhere—in a bedroom, at a new chapter—or was involved in the most insignificant exchange, these experiences were illuminated internally, became dazzling, were transcended by the approaching departure they implied so strongly that he ended up confusing them with himself and becoming lost. Of every new thing he discovered, he would say:

"My, my: so this is what I'm going to leave behind."

Translated by Ursula Meany Scott

MARC CHOLODENKO

from *Quasi una fantasia* (Almost a Fantasy, 1996)

Look look. Say eat after the word eating. Fish eat plane eats pedestrians eat fingers eat shoes eat. Listen listen look eating eat. Look look listen it's true you say it's true eating eats it's true. Because when we are silent, we can no longer eat, and when we eat things, we can no longer say eat after. But when we say eat after we ate what we say. But is it dangerous to say it after dangerous words. Are there dangerous words to say before eat? Are there words—large for example. Or after we are large. Fireplace eats. Look look listen if you say fireplace eats alone in the street over there so that others don't hear that you grow like the fireplace but quietly, if not the others hear you and see it and they see that it doesn't work. Say that you see it. Say it. Say it. Say it, I swear you'll see it, look say it just whisper chimney. Say it. Quietly. Yes, go on, say it. I'll just do that. Quietly, yes, go on quietly. Go on be nice what does it matter to you. It's not going to eat you. To make me happy. You'd do well to make me happy so why do you not say what difference it makes. Just one time. Quietly. Quietly. I do it for you. I'll just do it for you. Stop and say it if it bothers you. All right, stop. Stop I tell you. I want it more like this. Stop I tell you. Stop. That's enough now. Stop. Stop saying that. It's vulgar. I am not ashamed of you I never said I was ashamed of you only just saying that it doesn't seem like you. It is not you. I know well what is you and what is not you. Better than you yourself yes better than yourself. That is why I love you.

Translated by Lauren Messina

NICOLAS FARGUES

from *Le Roman de l'été* (Summer Novel, 2009)

All the conditions were fulfilled, yes. But John really felt that he was missing what was most important: the evidence, the urgency prerequisite to all this mise-en-scène. And if his desire to write was nothing but a vulgar, bourgeois whim? What was it, exactly, the *need* to write? He threw a last imploring be-trayed-lover's glance over his pages and pen, sighed, turned on his heel, and went back into the house, where the water must have boiled ages ago by this time. A minute later, he was back out on the terrace again. Everything was ready on the table. The sachets of Earl Grey were brewing in the teapot, and the mug was waiting. Turning his Bic over and over in his fingers, John idly scanned the horizon, conscious of the fact that he was absently daydreaming, passively wrestling with the mounting despondency he felt.

A fresh glance over the silent sheets spread under his nose made him real-ize how blinding their whiteness was in the glow of the midday sun. He put down his pen, got up from the chair, and went to find the sunglasses in the living room. When he came back, the table seemed to him slightly lopsided. Considering the irony of his gesture, he then sacrificed one of the pages he'd brought out in order to fashion a makeshift wedge, which he placed under one of the table legs. The level balance of the table having been reestablished now called for a further comfort: a cushion under his ass. So John got up again, swearing to himself that it was the last time he'd find a good reason not to get down to work, and came back with two cushions, the second for his lower back, now convinced he'd become the plaything of a perverse utilitarian mechanism that could only lead to madness.

Translated by Ursula Meany Scott

JEAN FRÉMON

from *L'Île des morts* (The Isle of the Dead, 1994)

It's been ten years already since I buried Clémence, and her radiant face, un-changed, still floats in the air before me. Sometimes I catch sight of her sil-houette at the end of a lane, wrapped in a large black shawl, one of her arms under the handle of a basket.

I have never tried to draw a portrait of Clémence. I don't believe I ever will. Once, however, I drew her back; I clumsily copied a drawing by Seurat, an old woman from behind with a basket at her side, moving away down a stony lane, a strand of hair escaping her chignon, a shawl over her shoulders. It's the shawl I recognized first, then the chignon with its strand of hair escap-ing, then her whole limping gait, the stones in the lane, I said to myself: it's Clémence. And yet all those details—shawl, chignon, basket, stones—were hardly fleshed out by Seurat, it's a little drawing done quickly, in pencil on a little piece of paper, it's a rough sketch, an idea quickly noted down, almost a stain on the creamy white of the paper whose grooves remain noticeable underneath the thick graphite that hasn't gathered in the little dips they form, so that the drawing seems striated with white lines, and these white lines il-luminate the drawing from within, giving it this vibration, this life it main-tains, to this very day, whenever we look at it, even in this bad reproduction, and which made me exclaim to myself: "It's Clémence." All Clémence's quali-ties were there, from behind, preoccupied, moving away, not speaking, busy only with her work of moving away, and the strand of hair, the chignon, the shawl, the limping over the stones, and the interior light of the grooves, it was Clémence. So I wanted to keep a trace of her, I could have cut it out of the book, stuck that image into a notebook, but aside from the fact that I've never been capable of making myself attack a book with a pair of scissors, the deeper reason I didn't bother was that I wanted to make this image my own. I made a copy, a clumsy one, but the clumsiness was required, it was the clumsiness that would make the difference between a lifeless copy of a drawing by Seurat and my Clémence, the Clémence I had seen in his drawing and who had never belonged to anyone but me.

From Georges Seurat I borrowed the strand of hair, the chignon, the shawl, the basket, the stones on the lane, the light of the grooves, his way of merging all of this into an almost formless mass; from Clémence, from the memory of Clémence, I borrowed her silence, her absence, the quality of her presence, which was precisely to be a silent absence; I trusted that my clumsiness would not betray my emotion.

Translated by Ursula Meany Scott

EMMANUEL HOCQUARD

from *ma haie* (My Hedge, 2001)

INTONATION

You will find, in any dictionary, the definition of each of the words that we use when we speak and when we write. The definition of the word *table*, for example, is written there, and it's the same for everybody. The definition of the word *goat* as well. We are all in agreement about the fact that the word *table* and the word *goat* do not represent the same thing and that when several of us are talking about a table, it's really a table we're talking about, not a goat. Consequently, it will never cross our minds to feed chestnut leaves to a table.

That said, other questions remain to be answered. Nobody learned to speak by using a dictionary. The dictionary comes afterward. Even if everybody is alike (See *commonplace*), even if everybody can refer to a dictionary in order to check or clarify the definition of whatever word, each of us learned to speak in a different context, even if those contexts were similar: in such a place, in such a family, at such a time, etc. It follows that, for each of us, the word *table* is colored differently depending on the experience we've had of tables, and according to circumstances, our character, our sensibility, etc. In other words, even if everyone agrees about the general and abstract (outside of any context) dictionary definition of the word *table*, in life, whether we like it or not, *my table* is not *your table*. Whether I like it or not, *my table* is made up of thousands of meanings (in every sense of the word), layered and interconnected, and your table thousands of others. All these nuances are *intonations*. And the set of *my intonations* of the word *table* and of *your intonations* of the word *table* mean that the word *table* hasn't the same global intonation on your tongue as it does on mine, under your pen and under mine, in your ear and in mine.

Consciously or not, anyone who writes knows this. He finds himself simultaneously with his *table-intonation*, linked to his history of tables, and the *table-word*, which he shares with everybody but which, as such, is perfectly opaque, abstract, a pure mystery. "Would I had seen a white bear (for how can I imagine it)?" wonders Tristram Shandy's father.

If everybody is alike, then everybody has experienced, at least once in their lives, the nameless fear when faced with the total opacity of a word. It's like suddenly having gone blind or finding yourself somewhere new or just as suddenly not having any idea where you are. Being lost.

Translated by Ursula Meany Scott

CÉLIA HOUDART

from *Les Merveilles du monde*
(The Wonders of the World, 2007)

He had an omelet with fine herbs for dinner. With his thumb he turned a fine shell that shone like porcelain around in the palm of his hand. He called Monica in Madrid. He thanked her for a self-portrait she'd sent him the evening before over the Internet. A self-portrait taken with her cell phone held at arm's length. Camera shake. Her clowning around. Then Igor suggested Monica come and spend a few days at his place over the last weekend in September for the preview of a collective exhibition being shown at the Musée de l'Elysée in Lausanne. She told him she really hoped to come.

As always, they were both quite moved, speaking with one another. And they were struck by the number of things they found to talk about in such a short space of time and saying so little about themselves.

The sun was setting. It was Igor's favorite time of day. Cyclamen clouds. Deep blue mountains darkening. A bird's singing. Then the night. Last evening of the summer. The people walking late in the streets.

Igor picked out a Taschen volume on Edward Weston from his library. He opened the catalogue to the page *Nude. Oceano.*

The next morning Igor swam close to the Veveyse Bridge. He moved forward, head turned towards the vineyards. The sky was clear, the water calm.

Nobody noticed his disappearance.

Translated by Ursula Meany Scott

PATRICK LAPEYRE

from *La Lenteur de l'avenir*
(The Slowness of the Future, 1987)

One night, something comes toward her from the back of the bedroom. Something she must have been waiting for and, having waited in vain, had most probably forgotten. Something very internal, very personal, which is returning from a long way off, as if it had become external to her, and which arrives so quickly now that she only has just enough time to become aware of it: *a promise*. A promise someone would have made to her when she was little and that reappears in a rush to her adult self. But the promise of what? Of being happy? Of getting married, of being loved, of having a child? She doesn't even know. She knows it's a question of all of those things and that it's something else at the same time, something bigger, more imprecise: a certainty that is all the more strong for not having substance, like the promise of a promise. She got up again. She went into the kitchen to open the window. She does the same thing in the bedroom, the dining room, and the air pours into the open rooms. There isn't a single light on anywhere. She sat down on the kitchen stool to drink a glass of milk. She wants to leave.

Translated by Ursula Meany Scott

MATHIEU LINDON

from *En enfance* (In Childhood, 2009)

There is something between his thighs, something that definitely belongs to him. Flat on his stomach, he can rub it against his bed and it's the first time such rubbing is so enjoyable. Soon comes a second, a third, an nth time, the pleasure doesn't wear off. Though he feels there's a risk involved. If his mother comes into the room while he's nervously and greedily engaging in this rubbing, he has learned to hide this fact at once; it's of paramount importance that she not catch on.

"What are you doing?" she asks, suspicious.

"Nothing," he says, getting up as though only a passing and already departed sense of lassitude had made him lie down.

It's the opposite of nothing. "Nothing" is when he's just hanging around, when he's playing alone at the games he invents so readily, when he isn't doing any work. And he never works once he gets out of school, and he has barely any friends—so nothing is all the time. And this thing between his legs is something, and not only that, something that will never leave him, something with which it's going to be necessary to cooperate.

This excrescence between his legs is a disturbing sort of pleasure. He had arranged his life in a bearable manner, he had found his niche in it, and all of a sudden it's no longer suitable. One can never be calm with this stuff hanging off of you. He rubs himself frantically, perhaps hoping that he might make it disappear that way, or simply because it's so good, a gentle and severe contradiction. He dreams of asses, of completely naked people. His mother can't suspect. In any case, he obtains a bolt for his bedroom door.

Suppressing his vice is a way of maintaining his taste for discretion. One day, however, in a bedroom with six boys at a holiday camp, he engages in his rubbing, lying fully clothed on a bottom bunk. He's sure that nobody notices anything, the same way that drug addicts can go get their fix in the bathroom ten times a day without ever considering that they're calling attention to themselves—as long as no one actually points out their strange behavior, confusing their habit with some form of bulimic masochism.

"Goddamn, did you see that?" says a boy who's pointing him out to the dormitory big shot when he's almost finished.

He's fully dressed; he knows that his behavior would seem reprehensible in the eyes of their maternal overseers, but why would other boys his age take up this accusation? The fact that he's different gives them reason enough. He fears being revealed, but it would be eye-opening.

"Leave him alone," says the big shot, with whom he gets on well, and the other boy obeys.

He feels that sexuality will be strictly a matter between him and his sex, that if only people leave the two of them alone he'll end up working things out to his general satisfaction. A friend tells him about using his hand, there's more to it than rubbing. And the way to do it, flat on your back, seems an affirmation, an assertion, a flaunting of one's self, almost a pretension. Rubbing himself lying flat on his stomach, sometimes semi-naked, like when he lowers his pajamas under the sheets, satisfies his urges for the time being; it's the best way to exploit his hard-won solitude. Education isn't his thing—he still has no thoughts about getting ahead.

Translated by Ursula Meany Scott

HUBERT LUCOT

from *Le Centre de la France*
(The Center of France, 2006)

When a thirty-seven-year-old woman walks beside an adolescent (I'm eighteen and a half) in a buttoned winter coat on the footpaths of la Muette beneath the large apartments overlooking the small Balbec railway line that follows le Bois as far as the Porte d'Auteuil, today I project a state of being which, controlling my meditation and these pages I write, moves me more than the account and even the register of strong feelings: in the spring of 1954, Trèfle arrives quite late in a corner of my Vieux Quartier that's cut out by a bistro shaped like a trapezium . . . I closed the door of the bedroom on which I read the large number 106 (for instance), she threw her black raincoat on an armchair . . . turning around from the door that I lock with the key, I squeeze her breasts under her sweater . . . she has nothing on underneath, I kiss her breasts free of their bra, see her shoulder in the mirror. Today it is probable that this WAS, and that on another absolutely identical occasion, she undresses so quickly that she is naked in the bed, the sheet pulled up to her chin, I will uncover her admirable breasts with their full nipples and then the top of the sheet outlines her pubis . . . It's possible that it was like that, detail for detail, but no detail constitutes an individual memory: whether in the past historic or present perfect, the tense is substituting for the imperfect: "They were happy."

Translated by Ursula Meany Scott

DANIELLE MÉMOIRE

from *En attendant Esclarmonde*
(Waiting for Esclarmonde, 2009)

A little book about nothing in particular that I might try to write while waiting for Esclarmonde, entitled *Waiting for Esclarmonde*, what would you think of that? Would it be a little silly? Totally silly? Or not as silly as all that?

These are the questions that I asked you one morning last January in an e-mail that never reached you because I didn't send it to you. I was still planning on telling you what I imagined my book would consist of when it suddenly appeared to me that it had entered into its *enunciation space*.

Only I didn't go over it another time in my head so that I could explain to you what is meant exactly by this improvised concept of mine: too many versions precede this one, this one is only one version of many, several precede it, all of which have more or less the same beginning; no more can follow, too many of these versions fail. Nothing particular is at fault, they just never manage to say who conceived of itself. Besides, haven't they already lost a ridiculous amount of time discussing the same word as "space," each in turn convinced that this "register," that it must be said—or if it is not "registered," then what?—for, one after the other, all eventually agreed that "register" is also metaphorical.

You will remember this lesson: when you see yourself entering—and, with you, the hope for a book—into a discursive space, you will not try to define what that space may be, nor why it may be called space, unless, at least, you wish to leave it in order to lose both your hope and yourself.

As for this discursive space, it will suffice for you to know that, being extremely narrow, it tends constantly to shrink, and that I myself feel the same *aber diese langen Mauern eilen so schnell aufeinanderzu* . . . effect as the mouse in Kafka's little fable.

Translated by Lauren Messina

BERNARD NOËL

from *La Langue d'Anna* (Anna's Language, 1998)

I'm not who you think I am. I don't know much about who I am, and if I did, would I truly be her? I do not, however, lack an identity. Instead, it overwhelms me, and tosses me out of myself. Perhaps I've done too much to have a face that is entirely my own. That sort of work has taken up all my time, I suppose. I certainly didn't think much about . . . I mean to say that I didn't think that my time and my face were connected. I believe that things are forced on us by the appetite that we have for them. I've never been mistaken about desire, most likely because for me desire takes the place of certainty, and consequently of will. I hesitate here, not because I doubt the correctness of this statement; I only fear not having properly explained myself, even though this suits me. I spoke often with the words of others, this is why they put me in charge of these words here. I spoke them so well. I also made sure to espouse them entirely. Otherwise, I would not be convincing. I enjoyed being identical to their meanings. I enjoyed this verbal penetration, because it was far more vivid in me than the other. I wonder if having sung first encouraged this intimate feeling, but it is not the voice, nor even the particular way that it vibrates in the body, but it is really the sense that I felt circulating within me, like a hot flash. I felt it on the condition (did I really perceive it?) on the condition that the words weren't my own. I mean on the condition of not speaking for myself but on behalf of the name that I constructed. By making this distinction, I am moving forward toward something that will tear me apart. Perhaps I will find in myself something that I had previously driven away. I wanted to be the Diva, and now I tremble at the thought of being nothing more than her. I lament that time in front of the mirror when beauty left me, leaving my face to the ugly, the vile, and the coarse, who threw themselves on me by pushing on the door of my skin. I watched it happen, then never saw any more as time slipped in behind the vast terrain that serves as my headshot. I have long been aware of this shift, which signifies the end of struggle, and the arrival of abandonment and repose.

Translated by Lauren Messina

VALÈRE NOVARINA

from *Devant la parole* (Before Words, 1999)

To speak is to experience what it is to enter and exit the cavern of the human body with each breath: galleries, unseen passages, forgotten shortcuts, and other pathways are opened; progress is difficult; incompatible paths must be traversed in the wrong direction. We advance by an excavation of the spirit, through an open struggle: to speak is to excavate within the underground of the mind. We who speak dig into our language, it is our earth.

Speech advances in the dark. Space does not extend, it is heard. Through our speech, matter is opened, it is pierced with words; reality unfolds inside it. Space is not the place where the body exists; it does not act as our support. Language takes up this space and holds it *before us and in us*, visible and open, charged, offered up to us, opened by the drama of a time in which we too are suspended. The most beautiful thing about language is that we pass with it. The sciences of communication tell us nothing about all this, yet we know this fact well enough through our hands in the night: we know that language is the *place where space appears*.

The flesh of our tongues does not bring us together, nor does it attach our feelings and our opinions to one another, rather it opens itself before us like a field of forces, like a magnetic theater. In its essence, speech is not human; there is nothing human about it; it is a whispered antimatter that makes the drama of the species appear before us. We look into it as we look into real matter.

Speech remembers, announces, and transmits; it traverses us and passes by us without our knowledge. Words are not manipulable objects or moveable cubes to be piled upon one another, they are trajectories, exhalations, crossings of appearances, they are *directives*, fields of absence, caverns, theaters of reversal; they contradict, they whisper. Language grasps nothing, it calls—though not to make something come, but to throw forth an extension and to make the distance between everything vibrate; it takes without taking, it separates and draws near.

Translated by Gregory Flanders

EMMANUELLE PAGANO

from *Les Mains gamines* (Childlike Hands, 2008)

I must have gone to sleep quickly.

A little cry from the room next door woke me up. A very strong little cry, I'm not quite sure how to describe it. A brief moan, but sustained, insistent. Little at the edge of my sleep, but very intrusive. A little cry breaking into my night.

I checked the time on the alarm clock on the bedside table. It was ten past two. Daylight savings happens during the night, so I didn't know if it was really two o'clock, or I don't know if it's now two o'clock. I don't know if the hour gained isn't actually an hour lost, because, if at three o'clock it's really two o'clock, where does it go, that previous hour? Where has it gone? And also, has it really gone? The minutes, the seconds, the time, I wonder where it goes. What happens between two o'clock and three o'clock. If something happens at ten past two, does it really happen, does it take place, and afterward, where has what happened gone, that worries me a little, the places of the things that happen during the change to daylight savings.

Immediately after the cry, I felt an ache in my stomach again, so much so that I believed I myself had let out the cry, I believed it had been mine. But no. I got up and the pain got duller, it ebbed. I didn't listen to it. I didn't listen to myself. I wanted to know the cause of that cry. I stroked the wall separating me from this moan until I found the place where the voice that had let out the cry was most noticeable. Because it was still audible. It was close to the ground, so all the better, I could sit down, my ear against the wall.

It was covered in warm wooden paneling. At least that was soothing. No words that I could hear.

I listened to everything. The voice, the breathing, the groans, the sound of bodies. There were other voices around the voice responsible for the cry. The maid's voice was the most unpleasant.

Afterward, she came looking for me.

Translated by Ursula Meany Scott

CHRISTIAN PRIGENT

from *Demain je meurs* (Today I Die, 2007)

You linger at the bedside. You don't dare sit on the chair. You don't dare say anything at all. You don't dare sniffle or take out a tissue at the risk of evoking the aforementioned thoughts. You don't dare push down the cowlick that keeps rearing up because of your shaking. You don't dare scratch anything that tickles on your skin, which is simmering in a stew of anxiety. You don't dare move your foot from where you've set it down. You don't dare cough. You don't dare clear your throat. You don't dare anything. You are wearing your armor of helplessness, you see. You fear any sound that could escape. What if it's the last time you speak to him? You're careful not to say a word that might hover there for eternity and never be silent. Sometimes he told you the fairy tale exactly as it's written: *Love, love, give me water / Love, love, give me bread / Love, love, give me life,* and you couldn't respond better than the Prince in the story: *Love, love, I have no water / Love, love, I have no bread / Love, love, my life has nothing to give,* and the conclusion would be the same as it is in the story: *Love, love, then I die.*

Then there is a mumbled sighing, a wisp of air. "Not much taste," it whistles. It leaves his mouth, saying, yeah, yeah. We don't see how, as his lips were already glued to the tubes as soon after they were able to stick to anything but themselves. This was done so that the relatives and the neighborhood couldn't see how his jaw falls slack because he can't hold it shut any longer. Nothing works any longer because Ankou has taken, or almost, his soul, which is already clawing at the feathers on the wings of the archangel as they glide through the light-years of language. We will fill the hole in his backside with cotton so that the rest of his soul doesn't leak out. Not much taste to what? He didn't specify, he just fell quiet again. Not much taste to anything, I suppose, no doubt. He clearly means: not much taste to everything; more: no taste at all. And nothing to drink. Except between the teeth: father, pay attention, otherwise you will soon be dead.

But if I look, though not too closely, not wanting to touch anything that still resembles flesh, I hear something, still, that comes out of him in the form of words, like the phylactery of the mouth of an angel, or a speech bubble in a comic strip. I listen to what he says, my father still strong for a little while yet, as if this is some last worldly revelation witnessed in person by me. He sighs it, and I hardly hear, "Yesterday I was born, tomorrow I die." Then he looks at his nails, closes his eyes again: good-bye. Nothing else but an echo, but the echo is me, repeating the word. He sleeps. You leave, walking on tiptoe. End of the visit, soon the end of everything. Afterward, turning on your heels, walking down the stairs, down the hall, drink in hand, fresh air, suburban smells, outside the ordinary. Get back on the bike, inhale the asphalt, pedal mechanically. And look elsewhere to sleep off your shame at not having known what to say, being sick and tired of feeling remorse about not knowing what to do, bathed in regret at not having dared, and drinking in the sorrow over everything that's been put together in the same pint and mixed well. Then the progression without rest, because the night that has fallen outside has fucked everything up and anointed your helmet with its soot of mourning. It has fallen over everything, both the setting and curtains in this last, or second to last, act. You pedal deeply in the cable lengths, you wrack your brain over the last word he whispered into your ear, and you repeat to yourself: never come, tomorrow, never come.

Translated by Lauren Messina

NATHALIE QUINTANE

from *Saint-Tropez—Une Américaine* (An American at Saint-Tropez, 2001)

In place of Saint-Tropez, there was water.

Since Saint-Tropez is already at the edge of the water, it's easier to imagine the sea in its place than in, say, someplace like Toulouse.

Yet Toulouse was once also the sea (you can imagine the rising tide, the sea rising to Saint-Tropez, covering its port, its houses, its steeple—though in reality the sea has sunk, withdrawn to take the place that it occupies today, staying more or less in place).

If we think about it, it requires an intellectual effort equal to the length of reflection to mentally picture a large amount of water instead of Saint-Tropez; to tell oneself that there is nothing but the sea where Saint-Tropez is; to chase away the photographic images in the back of one's mind. To chase away the lines of leaning houses, or the mythical allusions of glamorous, famous names, to substitute another, less familiar image: that of almost imperceptible waves when the wind is calm.

Thus, Saint-Tropez has been water.

Offshore, the waves are the memory of this (if they were to move one kilometer forward, Saint-Tropez would be underwater, we would not have had to imagine, one kilometer farther back, and fewer beignets would be sold during the summer. In principal, the waves do not recall that where we are now, they used to be).

Now, the waves call: a ten-year-old girl offshore in a dinghy; the gray coast-guard boat approaches; the arms of a coast guard, the hand of the girl, she is on board, the boat goes back to the port, where her mother anxiously awaits her on the beach. She removes her shoes and tights, has sand on her legs, and holds her daughter tightly to her chest. Then, entrusting her to a passing stranger, she walks toward the coast guard, thanking the man that she knows well, they kiss on the lips.

This is what we see when we see the sea at Saint-Tropez.

Even the fossil of a shell or a knife, discovered in the foundations of a home or on a hill a few kilometers further inland, does this speak immediately of the sea? Does this immediately bring the sea to mind?

Do we see the sea when we look at it?

I do not see the sea when I look at it, I see the mark of an animal in a stone. The imprint of an inanimate living thing. There, where before my eyes should be an image of water, I see a piece of hard earth.

Besides, we rarely lose sleep over trying to evoke the ancient sea when we gaze upon Saint-Tropez.

Translated by Lauren Messina

JEAN LOUIS SCHEFER

from *La Cause des portraits*
(The Cause of the Portraits, 2009)

What gift more precious, what treasure more sublime or more secret have I ever possessed than these suspended images and scenes that now represent the empty center of my life, the infinite enigma toward which I move without being aware of it, as if a thread, or a hint of a path, or a constraint of time forced me to survey, to weigh, measure, and manipulate all that material, all that matter and sediment out of which I am certainly made, soap bubbles blown through straws, their iridescent and milky whiteness carrying away with them tiny faces from a carnival of sugar.

Scenes, dim adventures, or rather last gasps from my life, as if I were a small machine rolling along, spitting out puffs of smoke as soon as an image appears in the sky, on the page of a book, on a street once traveled, or at the angle of that garden of which, to be honest, I have no memory; and all this because of these portraits that have raised the suspicion in me of fugitive resemblances that should be their last secret.

And how could all this have been possible together? These feelings that are so decisive and so violent, feelings that suddenly trap me in the body of a child, subject to the tyranny of its needs, the unreasonable impulses of its soul, the never-ending miseries, the exaltation before a beauty that has no cause and that is sometimes incarnated only in details, or in the tyranny of a god who insists on the impossibility of living at the same moment as me, or in me, no matter how docile I force myself to become: waiting, in sum, for a miraculous reconciliation of the world and my frail, personal universe. For I was only sure of possessing a flickering soul that simply alternated between pleasures more or less physical, more or less abstract. Certain as I was that the world's exteriority, its visible mechanics, consisted in reality of only a fleeting population and a few set dressings, a shapeless theater with a chaotic mise-en-scène shuffling around incoherent events that would simply cease to exist one day. The same day that my existence, my song, my infinite book, and my actions would finally join the sky and the earth, putting an end to this incoherent comedy in which no role had been written for me. This would certainly occur, as certainly as the war that had nevertheless molded an immobile and inexorable world had also ceased to exist as suddenly as a spring dries up, or when someone cuts off the water feeding a channel in a ditch. And, one morning upon waking, I saw that the war was no longer there. The spectacle, the roles, the innumerable tricks, the occupations, and the affairs had all disappeared; the world was empty, no cars stood in the streets, no cadence of footsteps, no bombardments, no airplanes rolling through the clouds, no impossible voyages. The world had become empty and, for a short time, silent.

Translated by Gregory Flanders

CHRISTOPHE TARKOS

from *PAN* (2000)

Literature holds itself up by its bearing, it is bearing, it doesn't hold itself to nothing, it holds itself to the good bearing that comes to it all at once, and, as such, literature holds on. In the grind of the its movements, unreadable by the its proper supported square form sits by insisting on holding onto its own pull. Literature is pulled in two opposite directions and possess the gift of opposing itself, it has the gift of auto-opposition, it has the gift of having pulled itself, to pull itself from all sides, from all four sides, it is a square, it is an elastic square, a square of elastic material, so it is said to have an elastic side, because it moves from each side, though remaining always attached to from the square to all that is not its side, to that which leads it to make its the form, there is much that is beyond the side, it is the largest part, by a good deal, clinging to everything that is and everything that isn't part of the side, it opens itself, it spreads its legs, it spreads its feet, it spreads its toes and it grasps, by spreading its feet literature is at its best, has the best posture, sitting, spread out, so that everything it can reach it does reach, and on all fours, it is already well disposed at all the places at once that hold themselves together, that have their feet on the ground, literature has its territory is territorial is attracted and is attached is held implacably has territory in all places, in all positions, it falls to its feet, it organizes itself automatically, when it opens, it always finds somewhere to open itself up, it hits all the right notes, it is an elastic square, by opposing itself, it supports itself always, by opening itself up, this is how literature holds itself, it is sat down pinned up and stirred up yes stirred up, supported by the crowd. Literature is literally dressed to impress in every sense.

Translated by Gregory Flanders

MARTIN WINCKLER

from *La Vacation* (The Vacation, 1989)

You are late. The car hurtles down the coast, and you have to slow down as you near the entrance to the hospital. The gate rises as you approach. You slowly pass by the guard booth. You lift your hand to acknowledge the guard. He responds by nodding his head.

You drive even slower down the lanes. You turn left, slow down further to allow a pedestrian to cross, and after a last, but brief, acceleration, the car stops alongside the sidewalk leading to Maternity, just below the service windows. You cut the ignition. The clock on the dashboard says 1:20. Your watch shows 1:18.

You get out of the car. You make sure that all of the windows are rolled up. You walk alongside the building until you arrive at the staff entrance. The door opens abruptly in front of you, revealing three women in deep conversation.

You enter. Posted on the door leading to the stairs, a written order asking to *Please Keep This Door Closed*. You obey, and in small leaps and bounds, climb the few steps separating you from the frosted glass double doors.

The hall is empty. As you pass, you glance at the fifty-year-old blonde who, behind her window, types in front of an emerald screen. You set off down the long white corridor.

At the other end of the corridor, the door is partly open. Hanging from the ceiling halfway down the hallway is an electric clock showing a quarter to eight, perhaps it's shown the same time for several days now. Two women are sitting, one at this end and one directly underneath the clock. One watching you approach, and one watching you move away. The one that you already have your back to is sitting in a deep armchair; she holds her round belly in her hands. The other is sitting straight up, her purse placed securely on top of her tightly closed thighs. She looks at you worriedly before resuming her surveillance of the door marked with the words *Family Planning*.

As you finish traveling down the path that separates these two women, you start to hear sounds of activity. Down there in the office, they're talking loudly; spoons clink against their teacups.

You step through the door and push it shut behind you with a single gesture. It closes gently, almost without making a sound. To your left, A.'s office is empty. To your right, J. and the other employees are having coffee and discussing children and knitting, houses and cars, large spaces and small meals. You present yourself in the doorway of the office.

"Hello ladies."

"Hello, sir."

"Hello, Bruno!"

"Are you doing well?"

"Very well, and yourself? Would you like some coffee?"

"No, thank you. Later."

Behind you, G. rises, steps away from her secretarial work, and with a look of fatigue, says in her drawling voice, "Hello, Bruno."

"Hello. What's the schedule?"

"There are three women today, and two consultations. Could you sign these prescriptions for me before you go? I don't have any more."

"Okay."

You take ten more steps. Before you turn left to commit yourself to the treatment room, you glance to your right.

The door to the waiting room is open.

In the doorframe, you see two legs, black high heels, fancy hose, and a leather skirt cut above the knees.

You slide into the treatment room. You close the door behind you.

Translated by Lauren Messina

JULIE WOLKENSTEIN

from *L'Excuse* (The Excuse, 2008)

This evening, I finally took a pill. So that the time would pass more quickly, so that it would be tomorrow already.

I am in the bedroom that was allotted to me, as a child, in this seaside villa that my mother hated so much. There is no hybridization in that dream of a house. My bedroom is only this bedroom, in no way mixed with any other. The tiny red flowers on the wallpaper are peeling off the damp walls in the same places, I bump my head against the iron bedstead with its white scrolls the same way I used to when I turn over. The sea is high and slaps against the seawall, noisier than ever here, on the island, the dunes keeping it all at a distance.

Around me, spread over the ground on the old wooden floor that has turned gray, generations of dust and sand clogged between its boards, on the little chest of drawers, also white, whose paint is flaking off, on the half-empty Formica shelves, where only cast-off books are still lying around— a biography of Marie Stuart from the children's "pink library" series, presumably a bowdlerized version, an illustrated *Famous Five* adventure (from when the series was in its decline), and, on the other bed, empty (my cousins are older than me, we never have to sleep in the same room), there are boxes everywhere. Beige. Rectangular. Closed. Without moving, without even turning my head on my pillow, I can read all their labels. So many epitaphs. So many gravestones. My father. My mother. Uncle Dick. Aunt Françoise. Juliette. Nick. Bruno. Mitchell, our old department head, the one who had "worked himself to death," according to that old alkie, Rodrigo. Samuel Strauss. And even Margaret Stone. The impact of the waves makes the box tops quiver slightly.

But this is not a funereal dream. The setting sun is still filtering through the slits in the shutters (they used to send the children to bed early, back in those days, long before the adults, gathered in the dining room below, drunk, would let out ridiculous squawks under their window in the illusory expectation of the green flash, the sun invariably masked by a cloud when it breached the horizon). And I feel fine, rocked by the vibration of the waves. The stack of boxes is less reminiscent of a cemetery than of Christmas presents piled at the foot of our tree—my parents' displaced, excessive generosity towards their only child: me. In the middle of these little, wet-sand-colored coffins, I am alive and I'm waiting to be given permission to open my presents. The best part of Christmas. The waiting.

Translated by Ursula Meany Scott

CONTRIBUTORS

MARIE DARRIEUSSECQ was trained at the Ecole Normale Supérieure, and holds a doctorate in French literature. A writer and a psychoanalyst, she published her first novel, *Truismes* (*Pig Tales*) in 1996. *Rapport de police* (*Police Report*), her thirteenth book for the Editions P.O.L, appeared in 2010.

GÉRARD GAVARRY lived for many years with his aunts and uncles in West Africa, far from Paris, where he was born in 1946, and where he lives today. Neither black, nor of mixed race, nor white (as he says of himself), he still hears the French of France over a background of tropical people and landscapes, over a backing track of other languages whose collective sound resonates in his ear as both utterly unfamiliar and beautifully harmonious.

JACQUES JOUET was elected to the Oulipo in 1983. He is the author of more than sixty texts in a variety of genres—novels, poetry, plays, literary criticism, and short fiction—including the novel *Mountain R*, which is part of his *La République roman* cycle, and was published by Dalkey Archive in 2004, followed by *Savage* in 2009. *Upstaged* will follow in 2011.

LESLIE KAPLAN was born in New York, but grew up in Paris, where she studied history, philosophy, and psychology. Her first book, *L'Excès–l'usine*, was published in Paul Otchakovsky-Laurens's collection at Hachette in 1982, and she was one of the first writers he recruited when he founded his own publishing house.

FRANÇOIS MATTON studied art and design in Reims. Thereafter, he became progressively more interested in what might be called "narrative drawing," and his books (most of which have appeared at the Editions P.O.L) blend texts and graphic art in intriguing new ways.

XABI MOLIA is a novelist, a poet, a comic book scenarist, a film director, and a professor of Film Studies at the University of Poitiers. His most recent novel, *Reprise des hostilités* (Truce's End), appeared in 2007; his most recent film, *Huit fois debout* (Eight Times Up), premiered in 2010.

CHRISTINE MONTALBETTI is novelist, playwright, literary critic, and theorist, and a professor of French literature at the University of Paris VIII. She has written five novels, including *Western*, which was published in English translation by Dalkey Archive Press in 2009.

WARREN MOTTE is a professor of French and Comparative Literature at the University of Colorado. His most recent book is *Fiction Now: The French Novel in the Twenty-First Century* (2008).

PAUL OTCHAKOVSKY-LAURENS is the founder and director of the Editions P.O.L. After studying law at the university, he apprenticed in the French publishing industry at the Editions Christian Bourgois in the late 1960s, moving to the Editions Flammarion in 1970. He went to Hachette in 1977, where he created a collection of his own. He launched the Editions P.O.L in 1983.

JEAN-JACQUES THOMAS taught at the University of Michigan, at Columbia University, and at Duke University before going to the State University of New York at Buffalo as the Melodia E. Jones Professor of French. His research interests focus on modern French poetry, linguistics, and Francophone literatures of the New World.

TRANSLATORS

GREGORY FLANDERS is a PhD candidate at Northwestern University and is writing a dissertation on the friendship between Franz Kafka and Max Brod. He has translated works of philosophy by the French philosopher Gilbert Simondon, and is currently working on a translation of a novel by Pierre Senges.

ERIC LAMB is a freelance translator from French. He recently received a BA in French and Economics from the University of Colorado.

LAUREN MESSINA is a literary translator and University of Illinois graduate. Apart from translating for several websites and nonprofit organizations, she is currently working on a full-length translation of Elisabeth Horem's novel *Le Ring*.

URSULA MEANY SCOTT is a literary translator based in Dublin and working from French and Spanish. Her translation of P.O.L author Claude Ollier's novel *Wert and the Life Without End* is due to be published in 2011. She holds an MPhil in literary translation with distinction from Trinity College, Dublin and was awarded a literary translation fellowship by Dalkey Archive Press in 2009.

BOOK REVIEWS

Tom McCarthy. *C.* Knopf, 2010. 320 pp. Cloth: $25.95.

Tom McCarthy's *C* begins as all good *Bildungsromane* must, with a child born, like David Copperfield, with a caul, and named, appropriately enough for this novel concerned with the early days of electronic communication networks, Serge ("surge") Carrefax. However, as with his first novel *Remainder*, McCarthy makes short work of dismantling conventions and readerly expectations, refashioning the narrative in a mode better suited to his preoccupations with communication, encryption, and the convergence between technology and the spiritual. Into his nineteenth-century frame, McCarthy inserts his own cipher text—fiction, here, is a form of encryption. As a "man without qualities," rather than a Copperfield, then, this avatar's short life embodies the historical transition from utopian confidence in technological progress to a hubristic idolization of the machine. In some sense, here McCarthy is the Ballard of the Zeppelin Age. Serge, like the modernists, has a problem with perspective and his chronic constipation is a metaphorical symptom of Europe's imbalanced humors. His golden-age Edwardian childhood is thus riddled with ominous portents, most notably (and with shades of Virginia Woolf's *Between the Acts*) in the staging of a pageant play of the rape of Persephone, with added brimstone pyrotechnics. His sister, Sophie, a science prodigy turned prophetess, sees the imminent war in omens from the natural world, and promptly doses herself with cyanide. It is this logic of pattern recognition that underpins the novel. From here, it hemorrhages overdetermined symbols and fragmentary allusions. However, the point is not, as Sophie's fate indicates, to crack the code: "the catastrophe was hatched within the network." *C* traces mid-century paranoia about information technology, seen in Pynchon, Gaddis, McLuhan and others, back to their point of origin. McCarthy uses his structure of failed transmission to explore the side alleys of modernity, just beyond the thresholds of history. [Jennifer Hodgson]

Eileen Myles. *Inferno (a poet's novel)*. O/R Books, 2010. 256 pp. Paper: $16.00.

Myles, now something of a wise yet still utterly hip elder of the poetry world, has always been the subject of her own poems, although never in a self-aggrandizing way; instead, she continually espouses a welcoming atmosphere, a narrative tone that enacts something of a friendship with her readers, even when it turns vitriolic and confrontational. And that same feeling of camaraderie is everywhere present in *Inferno*, as much a memoir as it is a novel. Here, she creates a chronology of excitement, one that spirals not into Dante's circles of hell, but into the miasma of social, sexual, and artistic awakenings. From the first stirrings of her literary consciousness in Boston to their full-fledged height in New York City, Myles takes readers into the depths of three decades' worth of being there—the art, punk, poetry, and lesbian scenes of the '70s, '80s, and '90s, and the often invisible yet palpably policed coterie line of each. Although her Inferno lacks an overt, guiding Virgil, there is in her circuitous looping of time the implicit guide of Myles herself, Myles in the present, the writer who talks directly about the construction of her book. And talk she does! Each sentence here darts forward with the rhythmic directness of speech, spilling exuberantly into the next, until it feels satisfyingly as if one is listening rather than reading. Ultimately, this is a coming-out story, not simply coming out as a lesbian, but also as a writer, as one who in her desire to be both present and to articulate her presence is almost damned to forever orbit the phenomenological world. As she makes clear: "Writing is just what I do to frame my longing. I replace myself. The longer I live the deeper it goes." [Noah Eli Gordon]

Georges Perec. *An Attempt at Exhausting a Place in Paris*. Trans. Marc Lowenthal. Wakefield Press, 2010. 72 pp. Paper: $12.95.

In Paris in late October 1974, Georges Perec sat for three days in various locations in Place Saint-Sulpice, observing and recording "that which is generally not taken note of, that which is not noticed, that which has no importance: what happens when nothing happens other than the weather, people, cars, and clouds." This turns out to be life itself: "A 63, an 87, an 86, another 86, and a 96 go by. / An old woman shades her eyes with her hand to make out the number of the bus that's coming (I can infer from her disappointed look that she's waiting for the 70) / They're bringing out the casket. The funeral chimes start ringing again." Such a work in anyone's hand would afford some anthropological interest; in Perec's always masterful grasp, it also proves greatly poetic ("The church square would be empty if the cop weren't pacing up and down it"). Despite his conceptual premise, Perec thankfully doesn't obey his guiding concept to the exclusion of everything else: the lists are fragmentary, casual, and, despite the book's title, not at all exhaustive. (One ellipsis occurs when a friend sits down for coffee; at other times Perec simply summarizes what he's seen.) He also meditates on his own meditations: "why count the buses? probably because they're recognizable and regular [. . .] the buses pass by because they have to pass by, but nothing requires a car to back up, or a man to have a bag marked with a big 'M' of Monoprix, or a car to be blue or apple-green, or a customer to order a coffee instead of a beer . . ." The result is very human and very moving; as in all excellent poetry, every mundane detail seems, upon consideration, vastly significant. Adding to this small volume's already immense worth is translator Marc Lowenthal's afterword, which locates the project in Perec's career and contemporary literature in general, and offers its own beautiful observations on how all writing is always done at a particular time, in a particular place. [A D Jameson]

Michel Sanouillet. *Dada in Paris*. Expanded and revised by Anne Sanouillet. Trans. Sharmila Ganguly. MIT Press, 2009. 640 pp. Cloth: $39.95.

When Michel Sanouillet's *Dada in Paris* first reared its head in 1965, it served as the seminal volume of Dada history, taking to task art historians who had "until recently excluded the Dada movement from their studies." Since then, terms like "avant-garde" have been regularly misappropriated as synonyms for "cool"; "Dada" for "nonsense." Dada still, and all too often, it seems, needs rescuing from the simplistic categories to which it is too easily assigned, and Sanouillet still offers an indispensible resource for doing so. As he reminds us, Dada is a rather significant endeavor: however "cool" in retrospect, its political portent, which Sanouillet emphasizes, should not be ignored. Although Sanouillet accounts for Dada's birth in Zurich and subsequent international dispersal, he argues for its preeminence in Paris, inextricable from the events of a brutal and unpredictable war, both politically and aesthetically (as a reaction against the lyrical "verbal and poetic excess" of so many WWI poets). In other words, Dada was far from nonsensical; it was a serious business, its antics the only sensible response to a mad world. Sanouillet details its rise (which he dates as starting in 1915) and fall into Surrealism (when taken over by André Breton in 1923, in what the author calls a "Dadaist apocalypse") with a depth and urgency that still holds today, paying particular attention to the literary output of enterprises such as *Littérature* and *391,* as well as to the personal relationships between its various young members. An impressive collection of letters between foremen Tristan Tzara, André Breton, and Francis Picabia serves as a kind of appendix, a reminder of the role these friendships played in Dada's output and eventual decline. "My dear friend," writes Tzara mournfully after a misunderstanding, "why are you forgetting me?" Dada's death was built into its very foundation, as implied in the book's epigraph by Tzara: "Must we assume that nowadays two deaths are needed—that of the poet and that of his era—for this consciousness to manifest itself in the form of a delayed rehabilitation?" Now celebrating its forty-fifth year, *Dada in Paris* has been fighting for Dada's critical inclusion since its poets were still alive; this long-overdue first English translation, nimbly composed by Sharmila Ganguly, just might be evidence that the time for Tzara's so-called "rehabilitation" has finally come. [Stefanie Sobelle]

Norman Lock. *Shadowplay*. Ellipsis Press, 2009. 138 pp. Paper: $13.00.

Storytellers remind us that data retrieval is really a kind of betrayal, that truth and meaning are elusive, and that we see our selves, our relationships, our surroundings, as if through curtains. Norman Lock's *Shadowplay* penetrates these diaphanous folds by casting light on the folly of irreconcilable love, the melancholic ache of nostalgia, and the burning yearning of art, of making something out of nothing. The art practiced here is *wayang kulit*: one form of the Javanese shadow-puppet theater. *Wayang* literally means "shadow" or "imagination," but can also mean "ghost" or "spirit." *Kulit* means "skin" and refers to the chiseled leather from which the puppets are made. It's from this marriage of skin and spirit, of body and soul, that *Shadowplay* comes to life. It's the story of master puppeteer Guntur's "impossible love, which overrules reason," for Candra, a village girl. Not unlike *Death in Venice*'s creepy obsessive, Guntur's infatuation leads to wild, wistful exaggerations of the beloved, in this case, the young girl's perfunctory retellings of her past. Lock's story is as much about a puppeteer's power to bring things to life, how this unravels and ruins him, as it is a reverie on storytelling where Guntur steps out "over an abyss with nothing to sustain him but an unwinding sentence engendering—by his skillful invention—another which, in turn, lengthened into its successor." Stories, for him "were only congeries of sentences, and the world . . . was a congeries of stories."

Swathed in darkness, Lock traverses liminal realms with glassine sentences reminiscent in form and substance of the like found in Gene Wolfe's and Ursula K. Le Guin's fiction, sentences you may be tempted to set off into line-broken verse. *Shadowplay* is another of the master locksmith's nested boxes whose evocative, ensorcelling prose will withstand multiple readings, especially if read aloud. [John Madera]

Matthew Roberson. *Impotent*. FC2, 2009. 166 pp. Paper: $13.95.

Beware the user of footnotes in fiction: you tread on well-trod ground, friend. Matthew Roberson bravely uses them and other textual devices in *Impotent*, his second novel, a short but potent collection of narratives describing the intersection of life and pharmaceuticals. Soulless jobs and colorless marriages and the enervating demands of childcare precipitate the use of a cabinet's worth of meds for the novel's characters, most of whom are identified by only a single bleak and faceless initial: L., C., S., F. Adding to the disaffected tone is the reliance on Maso/Marksonesque paragraphs and stanza breaks, which creates a wealth of white on the page and makes for a chilly atmosphere, a surprisingly effective way to convey the characters' alienation. Given all the disconnections on literal display, the footnotes and boxes and other textual disruptions aren't entirely a grad-school creative writing trick (kudos to Roberson for dodging that particular bullet). The logic behind what appears in the main text and what appears in the footnotes often seems arbitrary, reflecting the way the characters are no longer sure what they value—as M. puts it, "How little life requires motivation, or much thought. He found he didn't miss them." Roberson's interest in the Internet, first seen in his Sukenick-homage *1998.6*, continues here in the many copied-and-pasted descriptions of medications, which seems to be the characters' primary source of information about what they're ingesting in such heavy doses. (The public's worrying reliance on oft-transitory web sources isn't lost on Roberson: try looking up some of his cited sources and see how far you get.) The novel is at its most affecting in a brief endnote, set in a retirement home (and calling to mind B. S. Johnson's *House Mother Normal*): from birth to death, Big Pharma is there. [Tim Feeney]

Teddy Wayne. *Kapitoil: A Novel*. Harper Perennial, 2010. 320 pp. Paper: $13.99.

Teddy Wayne like James Joyce plays freely with the grammatical infelicities of the English language in his engaging first novel, *Kapitoil*. He incorporates incongruous words and phases into the voice of the main character, Karim Issar, a Muslim computer specialist from Qatar who immigrates to New York to work in the New York office of "Schrub Equities." Karim's goal is not only to improve his company's software, but also to master standard American English. We learn that Karim often feels "enhanced" (happy) in America but has to work on "rerouting his brain" and "stabilizing" his emotions as he solves various personal and cultural problems. When conversing with a Korean girl in a stifling dance club, Karim queries, "Is your tactile sense operating inefficiently?"—strange words that emerge from his math-obsessed brain. Wayne's knowledge of the way language shapes new realities comes from his experience editing English as a Second Language essays for applicants to American business schools (Joyce similarly taught foreign students at the Berlitz School in Trieste). Wayne filters Karim's sometimes incongruous usages, phrases, and ideas into the narrative of his novel, exploiting the resources of a new language: "Karimesque." But aside from the linguistic play and parodies of the business world, there is also a human story here, of an immigrant with strong family ties struggling to understand America: its baseball, music, art, Scrabble, and values. All in all, this novel—set before 2001—is about a more innocent time, when building a mosque, for example, in downtown Manhattan would not inflame the nation. A time when a computer specialist like Karim could tape-record his daily personal and business conversations in order to learn new jargon and business vocabulary, and get away with it. A time when a brilliant and rather funny and lovable character like Karim could be more fully appreciated in both life and literature. [Patricia Laurence]

Pierre Louÿs. *The Young Girl's Handbook of Good Manners*. Trans. Geoffrey Longnecker. Wakefield Press, 2010. 80 pp. Paper: $12.95.

Shoppers at modern "book" stores and hip urban clothing outlets know full well the current surfeit of coffee-table advice books—*100 More Ironic Cats that You Should Look at While You're Dying*—and their insipid cohorts. Pierre Louÿs, by way of contrast, is the real stuff. A straight drinking pal of Gide and Wilde, author of more mainstream works like *The Woman and the Puppet* (adapted to film by both von Sternberg and Buñuel), Louÿs labored away throughout his lifetime at so much elegantly refined smut (the delicately obscene was his stock in trade) that it was ultimately best measured by the tonnage—nine hundred pounds' worth, according to his biographers. This slender volume, itself comprising less than one nine-hundredth of that prodigious, prurient output, is nonetheless vintage Louÿs, consistently light and perverse and deliciously trashy—while also witty, insightful, and genuinely scathing. "For Use in Educational Establishments," his *Handbook* is rather obviously a send-up of social values both then and now hypocritical: "If you know that your mother is expecting her lover, do not hide under her bed, especially if you intend to jump out and shout 'Boo! It's me!' as he is coming in her mouth. You might make her choke." It also never surrenders the shameless pleasure of being erotic fantasy, eagerly imagining a world where sex is casual and constant, and where everyone—especially young girls—head off to bed each night well-fucked (where they engage in further frolics). This is just the book to give your niece—if she's a quiet, neat, straight-laced girl. [A D Jameson]

Gary Amdahl. *I Am Death*. Milkweed, 2008. 169 pp. Paper: $15.00.

The novella is regarded as a hybrid of the two more prominent forms of fiction, but novellas succeed when they are aware of their own duties and parameters. Gary Amdahl's intelligence, self-awareness, and philosophical acumen enable him to produce two tight, densely packed novellas here with grace and considerable wit. The opening piece, "I Am Death," is the first-person narrative of a journalist pressured into writing about Frank Fini, a legendary Chicago mobster. Fini is a colorful if largely silent character, more myth than man, and the narrator is carefully controlled by Fini's lawyer, who is even more colorful than his mafia contacts. Amdahl undercuts the clichés associated with organized crime with dark humor: opening a freezer door, the lawyer steps back and asks, "What's this guy's head doing in here still?" The narrator seems relatively unconcerned with the danger that surrounds him and is fascinated with this writing assignment, rather than perturbed by the immorality of those he writes about. "Peasants" is a longer, third-person novella about the infighting that weakens a small publishing company. The office is imagined as "a castle, and peasants are running in and out of the gate all day long with mock alacrity and devotion to the baron." We never meet the baron, the distant "founder" of the company, but we wince with pity and amusement as the so-called peasants slowly ruin their lives and those of others. (The protagonist nearly gets himself fired for brandishing a toy spear at a coworker as a way of diffusing tension). Amdahl's perceptive and hilarious writing places likable-if-flawed characters in contact with megalomaniacs—power-hungry men on the verge of insanity. The protagonists become weary of dealing with the maniacs, but continue their lives nonetheless, holding onto their convictions despite the scorn of ex-wives or the directives of the men in power. There is much more to know about these people, their work, and the worlds they inhabit, but Amdahl's restraint and keen sense of narrative arc are perfectly suited to the novella form. [D. Quentin Miller]

Martha Baillie. *The Incident Report*. Pedlar Press, 2009. 195 pp. Paper: $21.00.

There seems no better locale for peculiar characters and unusual goings-on than the public library, which happens to be the setting for Martha Baillie's most recent novel. *The Incident Report* presents itself in 144 brief, fastidiously observed reports that are all penned by Miriam, a faithful, rule-abiding employee at a Toronto public library and the novel's first-person narrator. A shuffled stack of vignettes tucked away in a desk drawer, these incident reports chronicle the mundane, as well as the peculiar, happenings of Miriam's life. Our narrator finds occasion to reflect often upon conversations with her coworkers, childhood memories of her father, and the deep passion shared with her cabby/painter lover, Janko. Baillie's writing is at its most confessional in these moments. The prose is rich with the *right* sort of details, depicting a very close, delicately rendered personal world. A humorous dichotomy exists between Baillie's very realistic dialogue and scene-setting, and the bevy of ridiculous and, at times, lewd and mentally troubled recurring characters (Suitcase Man, Lavender, Morality Man, the serial masturbator, the secret admirer who regards himself as Rigoletto in letters obliquely addressed to Miriam, whom he fancies to be his Gilda). All of these characters are essential players in this very human mystery—but one would be remiss to overlook Baillie's cleverly understated humor: a humor that becomes tragic, escalating in tandem with increasingly violent and unusual incidents as the novel progresses to its unraveling end. Rich with musical and artistic allusion, *The Incident Report* presents a unique and meaningful narrative delivered in a short, focused prose; a narrative of fragments that are interspersed with what Miriam might consider to be this strange business of living. [Andy Stewart]

Zoran Živković. *The Library*. Trans. Alice Copple-Tošić. Kurodahan, 2010. 111 pp. Paper: $7.50.
Zoran Živković. *Compartments*. Trans. Alice Copple-Tošić. Kurodahan, 2010. 159 pp. Paper: $10.00.

Zoran Živković. *Four Stories Till the End*. Trans. Alice Copple-Tošić. Kurodahan, 2010. 175 pp. Paper: $10.00.
Zoran Živković. *Miss Tamara, the Reader*. Trans. Alice Copple-Tošić. Kurodahan, 2010. 111 pp. Paper: $7.50.
Zoran Živković. *Amarcord*. Trans. Alice Copple-Tošić. Kurodahan, 2010. 99 pp. Paper: $7.00.

There is a strand of fantasy, sometimes called *fantastika*, whose practitioners— artists like Kafka, Borges, and Kobo Abe—give us stories, often short, that might be called modernist myths. Zoran Živković is of their number. The first thing we note in these five collections is the simple clarity of the language (translated from the Serbian by Alice Copple-Tošić). Like most of the preeminent practitioners of this brand of fantasy, Živković understands that language as unadorned and stripped down as possible provides a better backdrop for outrageous imaginings than would a more baroque style. When readers are confronted with, to offer just a few examples, a world where memories are bought, sold, and consulted like reference books; an online profile of a writer that includes books he has not yet written and years he has not yet lived; a string of compartments on a train each containing an impossible encounter for our protagonist; eyeglasses that erase text, vowel by vowel, consonant by consonant, from the books they are used to read . . . and one could go on: Živković's imagination is fertile. The quietness of the language keeps the fancy—which, at times, *is* baroque—from cloying. Working toward the same end is the rigor of the forms Živković employs. There is nothing duller than the facile surrealism one finds in books that are nothing more than one bizarre notion piled on top of another. Živković avoids this pitfall by establishing, in each collection, a theme, and, in his strongest work, developing these themes through repetitions of language and event in a way that gives his surrealism a satisfying shape. The stories in *The Library*, for example, the earliest work under review, are bound mostly by theme: each of the stories has to do with books and libraries. In *Amarcord*, each of the tales is titled after a literary classic: "Crime and Punishment," "Vanity Fair," "Great Expectations," and so on. In *Miss Tamara, the Reader* the stories turn, of course, around Miss Tamara's reading. Not least because they are the works with the most meticulous structures, the strongest of Živković's fantasies are the novella-length *Compartments*, and *Four Stories Till The End*. In the latter, for example, the titular four stories take place in different, but similar, chambers: a condemned man's cell, a hospital room, a hotel room, and an elevator. Each of the stories begins with a knock on the door, and in each case the door opens four times to admit four people who tell four different stories, each of which is intriguing on its own, but enriched by the resonances it shares with stories in parallel tales contained in other stories. Those who like their fantasy rigorous will relish the fiction of Zoran Živković. [David Cozy]

Eckhard Gerdes. *The Unwelcome Guest plus Nin and Nan*. Enigmatic Ink, 2010. 160 pp. Paper: $17.50.

One of the things one can never accuse Eckhard Gerdes of is not "testing the boundaries," "pushing the envelope" or, in this case, "challenging the margins." Clearly, in the tradition of the late Raymond Federman, of whom Gerdes was a major devotee, Gerdes's latest works, *The Unwelcome Guest* and *Nin and Nan*, pay a kind of homage to Federman in that these short novellas refuse to adhere to any kind of representational writing in favor of a kind of a poetic recalcitrance. The narrator of *The Unwelcome Guest* is fairly reliable in his unreliability, moving from place to place, thought to thought, and paragraph to paragraph with a kind of preconceived randomness that is not unlike what one will find in *Nin and Nan*, whose iconic thirteen chapters (lucky or otherwise) remind one of Burgess's iconic twenty-one chapters in *A Clockwork Orange*. Whereas *The Unwelcome Guest* is essentially narrative in nature, *Nin and Nan* is more dialogous, and shows how Gerdes uses dialogue in a way very reminiscent of Flaubert's method in *Bouvard et Pécuchet*, or Beckett's, on stage, with Vladimir and Estragon. An example of this kind of dogged dialectic is seen in Nin's comment to Nan: "Like Hadrian said: 'One brick at a time,' Nan. We must determine the vanishing points on either horizon and begin there, gradually removing a narrow strip of pavement from alongside the shoulder and then, eventually, from the road. This way, gradually, the road will become narrower and narrower until it just ceases to exist." Continuing down the road paved by his progenitors (Federman, Flaubert, Beckett) *The Unwelcome Guest plus Nin and Nan* is an admirable and charming addition to Gerdes's ongoing experiment. [Mark Axelrod]

David C. Dougherty. *Shouting Down the Silence: A Biography of Stanley Elkin*. Univ. of Illinois Press, 2010. 296 pp. Cloth: $40.00.

The late Stanley Elkin has a well-deserved reputation as a linguistic showman with an almost Shakespearean gift for high-flown diction, but to truly appreciate his accomplishments it helps to see him on the ground. *Shouting Down the Silence* is particularly good at delineating the mundanity that's required when forging a living as an experimental artist. As in Flaubert's famous dictum, Elkin strove to maintain a regular, orderly life so he could be violent and original in his work. In addition to being one of the most adventurous writers of his time, he was a career teacher and family man who was born where the avant-gardes usually wind up, New York, but moved to the Midwest and developed strong St. Louis ties. Dougherty describes various unsuccessful attempts to break into the lucrative realm of moviemaking, recurring conflicts with school administrators over salary, the difficulties of child rearing, and the increasingly complicated logistics of life with progressively worsening multiple sclerosis. Money is a main theme, which is particularly appropriate given that Elkin was nearly alone among literary writers in the high degree of focus he applied to the world of employment. His narrators revel in the detailed duties of job performance, and for all the verbal pyrotechnics that they display, socioeconomic realities are never far from their minds. Elkin may have been influenced in this by his admiration for his father, an energetic and charismatic salesman with a sharp eye for the bottom line. Not only did he inspire many of the robust figures in Elkin's books, his earnings (in the form of a timely loan) gave Elkin the bit of freedom he needed to launch his prose into the empyrean. Dougherty's own prose can't quite reach such lofty spheres, of course, but he's to be thanked for giving us a view of them. [James Crossley]

BOOKS RECEIVED

Baxter, Charles. *Gryphon: New and Selected Stories*. Pantheon, 2011. Cloth: $27.95. (F)

Burton, Gabrielle. *Impatient with Desire*. Hyperion Books, 2010. Paper: $22.99. (F)

Cixous, Hélène. *Zero's Neighbour*. Polity Press, 2010. Paper: $14.95. (NF)

Corso, Paola. *Catina's Haircut: A Novel in Stories*. Univ. of Wisconsin Press, 2010. Cloth: $21.95. (F)

Drummond, Roberto. *Hilda Hurricane*. Trans. Peter Vaudry-Brown. Univ. of Texas Press, 2010. Paper: $19.95. (F)

Duffin, Thor. *The Jefferson Project*. Steinwald Books, 2010. Cloth: $27.95. (F)

Engelhard, Michael, ed. *Cold Flashes: Literary Snapshots of Alaska*. Snowy Owl Books, 2010. Paper: $21.95. (F)

Farris, John. *The Ass's Tale*. Unbearable Books, 2010. Paper: $14.95. (F)

Germanacos, Anne. *In the Time of the Girls*. Boa Editions, 2010. Paper: $14.00. (F)

Grossman, Patricia. *Radiant Daughter*. Northwestern Univ. Press, 2010. Cloth: $29.95. (F)

Hall, Tina May. *The Physics of Imaginary Objects*. Univ. of Pittsburgh Press, 2010. Cloth: $24.95. (F)

Horack, Skip. *The Eden Hunter*. Counterpoint, 2010. Paper: $15.95. (F)

Kane, Jessica Francis. *The Report*. Graywolf Press, 2010. Paper: $15.00. (F)

Kramer, Frederick Mark. *Ambiguity*. Civil Coping Mechanisms & Journal of Experimental Fiction, 2010. Paper: $14.00. (F)

Lieder, Tim, ed. *She Nailed a Stake Through His Head: Tales of Biblical Terror*. Dybbuk Press, 2010. Paper: $12.75. (F)

Lopez, Robert. *Asunder*. Dzanc Books, 2010. Paper: $16.95. (F)

Martin, Chelsea. *The Really Funny Thing About Apathy*. Sunnyoutside, 2010. Paper: $13.00. (F)

Martin, Stephen-Paul. *Changing the Subject*. Ellipsis Press, 2010. Paper: $14.00. (F)

Myśliwski, Wiesław. *Stone Upon Stone*. Trans. Bill Johnston. Archipelago Books, 2010. Paper: $20.00. (F)

Nutting, Alissa. *Unclean Jobs for Women and Girls*. Starcherone Books, 2010. Paper: $18.00. (F)

Olsen, Lance. *Calendar of Regrets*. FC2, 2010. Paper: $22.00. (F)

Seidlinger, Michael J. *The Artist in Question*. Civil Coping Mechanisms, 2010. Paper: $14.00. (F)

Skemer, Arnold. *Sexptych*. Phrygian Press, 2010. Paper: $10.00. (F)

Sloan, Steven. *Deep Nights*. Cloud Dancer Publishing, 2010. Paper: $12.95. (F)

Somerville, Patrick. *The Universe in Miniature in Miniature*. Featherproof Books, 2010. Paper: $14.95. (F)

Steiner, Robert. *Negative Space*. Counterpoint, 2010. Paper: $12.95. (F)

Svoboda, Terese. *Pirate Talk or Mermalade*. Dzanc Books, 2010. Paper: $16.95. (F)

Trueblood, Valerie. *Marry or Burn*. Counterpoint, 2010. Paper: $15.95. (F)

Vukcevich, Ray. *Boarding Intructions*. Fairwood Press, 2010. Paper: $16.95. (F)

Washburn, Frances. *The Sacred White Turkey*. Univ. of Nebraska Press, 2010. Paper: $15.95. (F)

Annual Index for Volume XXX

Contributors

Šimko, Dušan. "Excursion to Dubrovnik," 2: 106–116.

Sloboda, Rudolf. From *Autumn*, 2: 101–105.

Suceava, Bogdan. "Daddy Wants TV Saturday Night," 1: 36–44.

Tarkos, Christophe. From *PAN*, 3: 133.

Thomas, Jean-Jacques. "Reading P.O.L," 3: 86–98.

Tsepeneag, Dumitru. "The Specialist," 1: 121–126.

Vilikovský, Pavel. "All I Know about Central Europeanism (with a bit of friendly help from Olomouc and Camus)," 2: 117–124.

Vlad, Alexandru. "The Double Rainbow," 1: 152–169.

Winckler, Martin. From *La Vacation*, 3: 134–135.

Wolkenstein, Julie. From *L'Excuse*, 3: 136–137.

Books Reviewed

Allemann, Urs. *Babyfucker*, 1: 263–264. (Jeremy M. Davies)

Amdahl, Gary. *I Am Death*, 3: 149. (D. Quentin Miller)

Auster, Paul. *Invisible*, 2: 147–148. (Robert L. McLaughlin)

Baillie, Martha. *The Incident Report*, 3: 150. (Andy Stewart)

Balzac, Honoré de. *Treatise on Elegant Living*, 2: 170. (Mark Axelrod)

Bergounioux, Pierre. *Une chambre en Hollande*, 2: 146–147. (Warren Motte)

Buckeye, Robert. *Left*, 2: 166–167. (Andy Stewart)

Buzzati, Dino. *Poem Strip*, 1: 259. (Jamie Richards)

Caponegro, Mary. *All Fall Down*, 1: 250–251. (Robert L. McLaughlin)

Castellanos Moya, Horacio. *Dance with Snakes*, 1: 252–253. (James Crossley)

Cotner, Jon and Andy Fitch. *Ten Walks / Two Talks*, 2: 163–164. (Amanda DeMarco)

Coutinho, Domício. *Duke, the Dog Priest*, 2: 151–152. (Joseph Dewey)

Daive, Jean. *Under the Dome: Walks with Paul Celan*, 1: 247–248. (Robert Glick)

Daudet, Alphonse. *Artists' Wives*, 1: 265–266. (Nicholas Birns)

Dougherty, David C. *Shouting Down the Silence: A Biography of Stanley Elkin*, 3: 153–154. (James Crossley)

Douglas, Norman. *Some Limericks*, 1: 267–268. (Michael Kelly)

Edwards, Ken. *Nostalgia for Unknown Cities*, 2: 154. (A D Jameson)

Evenson, Brian. *Fugue State*, 2: 165–166. (Richard Kalich)

Federici, Federico. *Translation as Stylistic Evolution: Italo Calvino: Creative Translator of Raymond Queneau*, 2: 169. (Scott Esposito)

Finger, Anne. *Call Me Ahab*, 1: 264–265. (Jeff Bursey)

Gerdes, Eckhard. *The Unwelcome Guest plus Nin and Nan*, 3: 152–153. (Mark Axelrod)

Gombrowicz, Witold. *Pornografia*, 2: 148–149. (Michael Pinker)

Gracq, Julien. *A Dark Stranger*, 2: 159–160. (Stephen Sparks)

Grandbois, Peter. *The Arsenic Lobster: A Hybrid Memoir*, 1: 261. (Pedro Ponce)

Grossman, Edith. *Why Translation Matters*, 2: 168–169. (Rhett McNeil)

Handke, Peter. *Don Juan: His Own Version*, 2: 153–154. (John Madera)

Hofmannsthal, Hugo von. *The Whole Difference*, 2: 149–150. (Lily Hoang)

Hunt, Laird. *Ray of the Star*, 2: 156–157. (Joseph Dewey)

Iossel, Mikhail and Jeff Parker, eds. *Rasskazy: New Fiction From a New Russia*, 1: 260. (Michael Pinker)

Jaffe, Harold. *Anti-Twitter*, 2: 161–162. (Gary Lain)

Josipovici, Gabriel. *After & Making Mistakes*, 1: 258. (Jeff Waxman)

Karapanou, Margarita. *Kassandra and the Wolf*, 1: 255–256. (Joseph Dewey)

—. *Rien Ne Va Plus*, 1: 256. (Joseph Dewey)

Kiteley, Brian. *The River Gods*, 1: 262–263. (Martin Riker)

Kleist, Heinrich von. *Selected Prose*, 1: 253–254. (Joao Ribas)

Kolloen, Ingar Sletten. *Knut Hamsun: Dreamer and Dissenter*, 1: 266–267. (Stephen Sparks)

Lennon, J. Robert. *Pieces for the Left Hand*, 1: 261–262. (John Lingan)

Lock, Norman. *Shadowplay*, 3: 145–146. (John Madera)

Lopez, Robert. *Kamby Bolongo Mean River*, 2: 164–165. (Mike Meginnis)

Louÿs, Pierre. *The Young Girl's Handbook of Good Manners*, 3: 148. (A D Jameson)

Masino, Paola. *Birth and Death of the Housewife*, 2: 155–156. (Jamie Richards)

McCarthy, Tom. *C*, 3: 141–142. (Jennifer Hodgson)

Morand Paul. *Hecate and Her Dogs*, 2: 157–158. (Jeff Waxman)

Myles, Eileen. *Inferno (a poet's novel)*, 3: 142–143. (Noah Eli Gordon)

Nerval, Gérard de. *The Salt Smugglers: History of the Abbé de Bucquoy*, 1: 257. (Shir Alon)

Ohle, David. *Boons & The Camp*, 1: 251–252. (A D Jameson)

Olsen, Lance. *Head in Flames*, 2: 150–151. (Peter Grandbois)

Oster, Christian. *Trois Hommes seuls*, 1: 245–246. (Warren Motte)

Pamuk, Orhan. *The Museum of Innocence*, 1: 248–249. (James Crossley)

Perec, Georges. *An Attempt at Exhausting a Place in Paris*, 3: 143–144. (A D Jameson)

Powell, Padgett. *The Interrogative Mood*, 1: 254. (Scott Esposito)

Powers, Richard. *Generosity*, 1: 249–250. (Stefanie Sobelle)

Roberson, Matthew. *Impotent*, 3: 146–147. (Tim Feeney)

Rosales, Guillermo. *The Halfway House*, 1: 255. (Thomas McGonigle)

Sanouillet, Michel. *Dada in Paris*, 3: 144–145. (Stefanie Sobelle)

Shawn, Wallace. *Essays*, 2: 167–168. (A D Jameson)

Sorrentino, Gilbert. *The Abyss of Human Illusion*, 1: 246–247. (Jeremy M. Davies)

Tokarczuk, Olga. *Primeval and Other Times*, 2: 155. (Jeff Bursey)

Unrue, Jane. *Life of a Star*, 2: 162–163. (Pedro Ponce)

Waterhouse, Peter. *Language Death Night Outside*, 2: 152–153. (Tim Feeney)

Wayne, Teddy. *Kapitoil: A Novel*, 3: 147–148. (Patricia Laurence)

Zambreno, Kate. *O Fallen Angel*, 2: 158–159. (Patricia Laurence)

Živković, Zoran. *Amarcord*, 3: 150–152. (David Cozy)

—. *Compartments*, 3: 150–152. (David Cozy)

—. *Four Stories Till the End*, 3: 150–152. (David Cozy)

—. *The Library*, 3: 150–152. (David Cozy)

—. *Miss Tamara, the Reader*, 3: 150–152. (David Cozy)

Zornoza, Andrew. *Where I Stay*, 2: 160–161. (Michelle Tupko)

DELILLO FIEDLER GASS PYNCHON
University of Delaware Press
Collections on Contemporary Masters

UNDERWORDS
Perspectives on Don
DeLillo's *Underworld*

Edited by Joseph Dewey, Steven G. Kellman, and Irving Malin

Essays by Jackson R. Bryer, David Cowart, Kathleen Fitzpatrick, Joanne Gass, Paul Gleason, Donald J. Greiner, Robert McMinn, Thomas Myers, Ira Nadel, Carl Ostrowski, Timothy L. Parrish, Marc Singer, and David Yetter

$39.50

INTO *THE TUNNEL*
Readings of Gass's
Novel

Edited by Steven G. Kellman and Irving Malin

Essays by Rebecca Goldstein, Donald J. Greiner, Brooke Horvath, Marcus Klein, Jerome Klinkowitz, Paul Maliszewski, James McCourt, Arthur Saltzman, Susan Stewart, and Heide Ziegler

$35.00

LESLIE FIEDLER
AND AMERICAN
CULTURE

Edited by Steven G. Kellman and Irving Malin

Essays by John Barth, Robert Boyers, James M. Cox, Joseph Dewey, R.H.W. Dillard, Geoffrey Green, Irving Feldman, Leslie Fiedler, Susan Gubar, Jay L. Halio, Brooke Horvath, David Ketterer, R.W.B. Lewis, Sanford Pinsker, Harold Schechter, Daniel Schwarz, David R. Slavitt, Daniel Walden, and Mark Royden Winchell

$36.50

PYNCHON AND
MASON & DIXON

Edited by Brooke Horvath and Irving Malin

Essays by Jeff Baker, Joseph Dewey, Bernard Duyfhuizen, David Foreman, Donald J. Greiner, Brian McHale, Clifford S. Mead, Arthur Saltzman, Thomas H. Schaub, David Seed, and Victor Strandberg

$39.50

ORDER FROM ASSOCIATED UNIVERSITY PRESSES
2010 Eastpark Blvd., Cranbury, New Jersey 08512
PH 609-655-4770   FAX 609-655-8366   E-mail AUP440@ aol.com

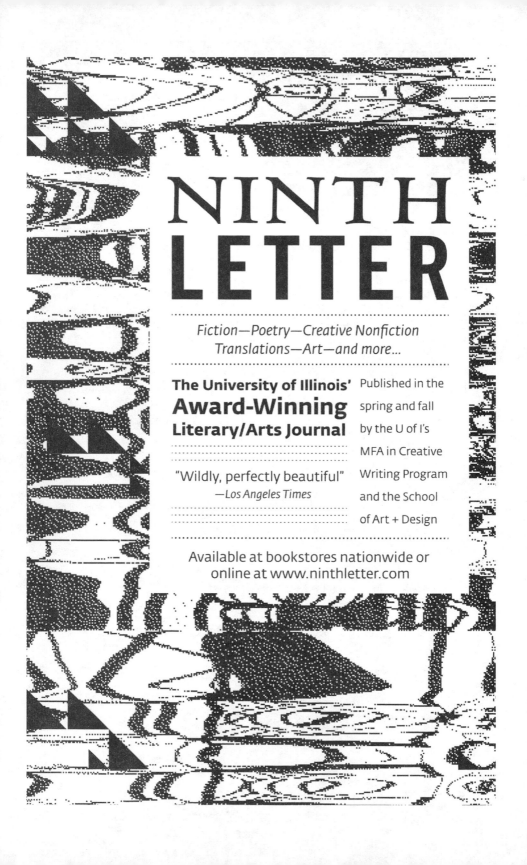

Dalkey Archive
Scholarly Series

Available Now

When Blackness Rhymes with Blackness
ROWAN RICARDO PHILLIPS

A Community Writing Itself:
Conversations with Vanguard Writers of the Bay Area
SARAH ROSENTHAL, ED.

Aidan Higgins:
The Fragility of Form
NEIL MURPHY, ED.

Nicholas Mosley's Life and Art:
A Biography in Six Interviews
SHIVA RAHBARAN

The Subversive Scribe:
Translating Latin American Fiction
SUZANNE JILL LEVINE

Intersections:
Essays on Richard Powers
STEPHEN J. BURN AND PETER DEMPSEY, EDS.

Phantasms of Matter
in Gogol (and Gombrowicz)
MICHAL OKLOT

Translation in Practice:
A Symposium
GILL PAUL, ED.

Energy of Delusion:
A Book on Plot
VIKTOR SHKLOVSKY

In *When Blackness Rhymes with Blackness*, Rowan Ricardo Phillips pushes African-American poetry to its limits by unraveling "our desire to think of African-American poetry as African-American poetry." Phillips reads African-American poetry as inherently allegorical and thus a successful shorthand for the survival of a poetry but unsuccessful shorthand for the sustenance of its poems. Arguing in favor of the counterintuitive imagination, Phillips demonstrates how these poems tend to refuse their logical insertion into a larger vision and instead dwell indefinitely at the crux between poetry and race, where, when blackness rhymes with blackness, it is left for us to determine whether this juxtaposition contains a vital difference or is just mere repetition.

When Blackness Rhymes with Blackness

ROWAN RICARDO PHILLIPS

Dalkey Archive Scholarly Series
Literary Criticism
$25.95 / paper
ISBN: 978-1-56478-583-1

when
blackness
rhymes
with blackness

ROWAN RICARDO PHILLIPS

Rowan Ricardo Phillips's essays, poems, and translations have appeared in numerous publications. He is also the author of *The Ground* (2010). He has taught at Harvard, Columbia, and is currently Associate Professor of English and Director of the Poetry Center at Stony Brook University.

A Community Writing Itself features internationally respected writers Michael Palmer, Nathaniel Mackey, Leslie Scalapino, Brenda Hillman, Kathleen Fraser, Stephen Ratcliffe, Robert Glück, and Barbara Guest, as well as important younger writers Truong Tran, Camille Roy, Juliana Spahr, and Elizabeth Robinson. The book fills a major gap in contemporary poetics, focusing on one of the most vibrant experimental writing communities in the nation. The writers discuss vision and craft, war and peace, race and gender, individuality and collectivity, and the impact of the Bay Area on their work.

A Community
Writing Itself
Conversations
with Vanguard
Writers of the
Bay Area

Sarah Rosenthal in conversation with:
Michael Palmer Nathaniel Mackey Leslie Scalapino
Brenda Hillman Kathleen Fraser Stephen Ratcliffe
Robert Glück Barbara Guest Truong Tran
Camille Roy Juliana Spahr Elizabeth Robinson

A Community Writing Itself:

Conversations with Vanguard Writers of the Bay Area

SARAH ROSENTHAL, ED.

Dalkey Archive Scholarly Series
Literature
$29.95 / paper
ISBN: 978-1-56478-584-8

"Sarah Rosenthal's interviews with some of the most engaging and important American poets of the time, all working in the Bay Area, provide vivid commentary on the state of the art and some of the most useful commentary available on the work of each individual writer."

—Charles Bernstein

Drawing together a wide range of focused critical commentary and observation by internationally renowned scholars and writers, this collection of essays offers a major reassessment of Aidan Higgins's body of work almost fifty years after the appearance of his first book, *Felo de Se*. Authors like Annie Proulx, John Banville, Derek Mahon, Dermot Healy, and Higgins himself, represented by a previously uncollected essay, offer a variety of critical and creative commentaries, while scholars such as Keith Hopper, Peter van de Kamp, George O'Brien, and Gerry Dukes contribute exciting new perspectives on all aspects of Higgins's writing. This collection confirms the enduring significance of Aidan Higgins as one of the major writers of our time, and also offers testament that Higgins's work is being rediscovered by a new generation of critics and writers.

Aidan Higgins:
The Fragility of Form

NEIL MURPHY, ED.

Dalkey Archive Scholarly Series
Literary Criticism
$29.95 / paper
ISBN: 978-1-56478-562-6

AIDAN HIGGINS:
THE FRAGILITY
OF FORM

edited by Neil Murphy
with essays from

ANNIE PROULX
JOHN BANVILLE
DERMOT HEALY
DEREK MAHON
GERRY DUKES
KEITH HOPPER
GEORGE O'BRIEN
PETER VAN DE KAMP
& AIDAN HIGGINS

Neil Murphy has previously taught at the University of Ulster and the American University of Beirut, and is currently Associate Professor of Contemporary Literature at NTU, Singapore. He is the author of several books on Irish fiction and contemporary literature and has published numerous articles on contemporary Irish fiction, on postmodernism, and on Aidan Higgins. He is currently writing a book on contemporary fiction and aesthetics.

The son of Sir Oswald Mosley, founder of the British Union of Fascists in the 1930s, and himself the inheritor of a noble title, Nicholas Mosley nonetheless fought bravely for Britain during World War II and became a tireless anti-apartheid campaigner thereafter, finding little sense in living the "hypocritical" life of a British aristocrat . . . and yet his numerous extramarital affairs came to shake not only the foundations of his marriage to his first wife, Rosemary, but also his growing sense of himself as a religious man.

The present biography is written in the form of six interviews, each focusing upon one aspect of Mosley's life—from his childhood and experiences as a young man, up to his reflections on religion, science, philosophy, and their impact on the political and ideological developments of our time.

Nicholas Mosley's Life and Art

a biography in six interviews
by shiva rahbaran

Nicholas Mosley's Life and Art:
A Biography in Six Interviews

SHIVA RAHBARAN

Dalkey Archive Scholarly Series
Literary Criticism
$25.95 / paper
ISBN: 978-1-56478-564-0

"Fascinating—Nicholas Mosley is the world's most brilliant conversationalist and this book catches the flavour of that."
—A. N. Wilson

To most of us, "subversion" means political subversion, but *The Subversive Scribe* is about collaboration not with an enemy, but with texts and between writers. Though Suzanne Jill Levine is the translator of some of the most inventive and revolutionary Latin American authors of the twentieth century—including Julio Cortázar, G. Cabrera Infante, Manuel Puig, and Severo Sarduy—here she considers the act of translation itself to be a form of subversion. Rather than regret translation's shortcomings, Levine stresses how translation is itself a creative act, unearthing a version lying dormant beneath an original work, and animating it, like some mad scientist, in order to create a text illuminated and motivated by the original. In *The Subversive Scribe*, one of our most versatile and creative translators gives us an intimate and entertaining overview of the tricky relationships lying behind the art of literary translation.

The Subversive Scribe:
Translating Latin American Fiction

SUZANNE JILL LEVINE

Dalkey Archive Scholarly Series
Literary Criticism
$13.95 / paper
ISBN: 978-1-56478-563-3

"A continually lively and very generous book, full of lore and such a vivid and just account of how complex a process good writing is."
SUSAN SONTAG

THE SUBVERSIVE SCRIBE
Translating Latin American Fiction
Suzanne Jill Levine

"A fascinating glimpse into the mental gyrations of a first-class literary translator at work."
—Clifford Landers, *Latin American Research Review*

Since his first novel was published in 1985, Richard Powers has assembled a body of work whose intellectual breadth and imaginative energy bears comparison with that of any writer working today. *Intersections: Essays on Richard Powers* pays tribute to that achievement by collecting seventeen essays—by leading literary critics, philosophers, and a novelist—each of which offers important insights into Powers's narrative craft and the intellectual grids that underlie his work. Powers's novels are distinguished by both their multiple narrative forms and their sophisticated synthesis of diverse fields of knowledge; to attempt to adequately address this range, the contributors to this volume mix their study of Powers's narrative innovations with eclectic interdisciplinary perspectives, which range from photography and systems theory to ecocriticism and neuroscience. The volume concludes with an essay by Powers himself.

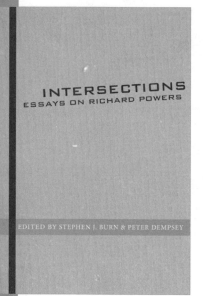

Intersections:
Essays on Richard Powers

STEPHEN J. BURN
& PETER DEMPSEY, EDS.

Dalkey Archive Scholarly Series
Literary Criticism
$29.95 / paper
ISBN: 978-1-56478-508-4

Contributors: Jon Adams, Sven Birkerts, Stephen J. Burn, David Cowart, Anca Cristofovici, Daniel C. Dennett, Joseph Dewey, Charles B. Harris, Scott Hermanson, Jenell Johnson, Bruno Latour, Barry Lewis, Paul Maliszewski, Richard Powers, Carter Scholz, Trey Strecker, Joseph Tabbi, and Patti White.

An investigation into the problem of art and matter in the work of Nikolai Gogol, and, indirectly, into the Neoplatonic tradition in Russian literature, *Phantasms of Matter* constitutes a rigorous examination of Gogol's "image of matter," as well as an attempt to enumerate the rules of its construction. After developing an artistic language corresponding to the Neoplatonic discourse on matter, Gogol subsequently abandoned literature; yet this transposition of the Neoplatonic problem has recurred frequently in Russian and Slavic literature following his death. Oklot therefore extends this investigation into the work of the Polish author Witold Gombrowicz, allowing unique parallels to be drawn between the writings of these two giants of world literature.

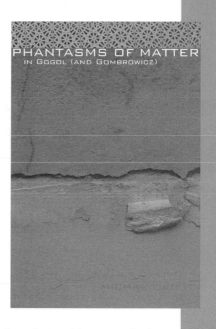

Phantasms of Matter
in Gogol (and Gombrowicz)

MICHAL OKLOT

Dalkey Archive Scholarly Series
Literary Criticism
$34.95 / paper
ISBN: 978-1-56478-494-0

"Combining complex philosophical analysis with uncannily intelligent close readings, Oklot provides strikingly new interpretations of the work of Gogol and Gombrowicz while simultaneously focusing attention on literary manifestations of new-Platonic thought. *Phantasms of Matter* is a tour de force."
—Andrew Wachtel, Northwestern University

Though translation is a vital part of any vibrant literary culture, no practical guide to the process of translating foreign works into English and preparing them for publication has yet been made available to prospective translators, editors, or readers. In February 2008, editors and translators from the US and UK came together at the British Council in London to discuss "best practices" for the translation of literary works into English. This volume comprises the results of that meeting—a collection of summaries, suggestions, and instructions from leading literary translators and publishers. It is intended as an introduction, the first in an ongoing series of documents to be published by Dalkey Archive Press that will address the challenges faced by translators, publishers, reviewers, and readers of literary translations.

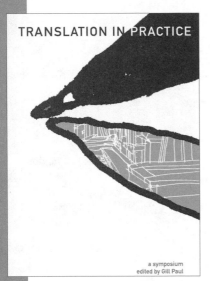

TRANSLATION IN PRACTICE

a symposium
edited by Gill Paul

Translation in Practice:
A Symposium

GILL PAUL, ED.

Dalkey Archive Scholarly Series
Literary Criticism
$13.95 / paper
ISBN: 978-1-56478-548-0

Contributors: Ros Schwartz (translator, director of the British Translators' Association), Euan Cameron (translator), Rebecca Carter (editor, Random House), Christina Thomas (freelance editor, publisher of *Editing Matters*), Martin Riker (associate director, Dalkey Archive Press), and numerous other translators, editors, and publishers.

One of the greatest literary minds of the twentieth century, Viktor Shklovsky writes the critical equivalent of what Ross Chambers calls "loiterature"—writing that roams, playfully digresses, moving freely between the literary work and the world. In *Energy of Delusion,* a masterpiece that Shklovsky worked on over thirty years, he turns his unique critical sensibility to Tolstoy's life and novels, applying the famous "formalist method" he invented in the 1920s to Tolstoy's massive body of work, and at the same time taking Tolstoy (as well as Boccaccio, Pushkin, Chekhov, Dostoevsky, and Turgenev) as a springboard to consider the devices of literature—how novels work and what they do.

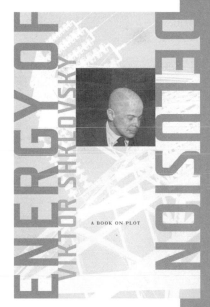

Energy of Delusion:
A Book on Plot

VIKTOR SHKLOVSKY
TRANSLATION BY
SHUSHAN AVAGYAN

Dalkey Archive Scholarly Series
Literary Criticism
$14.95 / paper
ISBN: 978-1-56478-426-1

"A rambling, digressive stylist, Shklovsky throws off brilliant aperçus on every page . . . Like an architect's blueprint, [he] lays bare the joists and studs that hold up the house of fiction."
—Michael Dirda, *Washington Post*

"Perhaps because he is such an unlikely Tolstoyan, Viktor Shklovsky's writing on Tolstoy is always absorbing and often brilliant."
—*Russian Review*

ORDER FORM

Individuals may use this form to subscribe to the *Review of Contemporary Fiction* or to order back issues of the *Review* and Dalkey Archive titles at a discount (see below for details).

Title   ISBN   Quantity   Price

_____

_____

_____

_____

_____

_____

Subtotal _____

Less Discount _____
(10% for one book, 20% for two or more books, and
25% for Scholarly titles advertised in this issue)
Subtotal _____

Plus Postage _____
(U.S. $3 + $1 per book; foreign $7 + $5 per book)

1 Year Individual Subscription to the **Review** _____
($17 U.S.; $22.60 Canada; $32.60 all other countries)

Total _____

Mailing Address _____

_____

_____

_____

Credit card payment   ☐ Visa   ☐ Mastercard

Acct. # _____   Exp. date _____

Name on card _____   Phone # _____

Billing zip code _____

Please make checks (in U.S. dollars only) payable to *Dalkey Archive Press.*

mail or fax this form to: Dalkey Archive Press, University of Illinois, 1805 S. Wright Street, MC-011, Champaign, IL 61820
fax: 217.244.9142 tel: 217.244.5700